# Grace and Gratitude

## SPIRITUALITY IN MARTIN LUTHER

EDITED AND WITH COMMENTARY BY
*Roger Haight, SJ, Alfred Pach III,*
and *Amanda Avila Kaminski*

FORDHAM UNIVERSITY PRESS   NEW YORK 2022

This series has been generously supported by a
theological education grant from the E. Rhodes
and Leona B. Carpenter Foundation.

Selection from Luther's *Lectures on Galatians* is reprinted
from *Luther's Works, Volume 26: Lectures on Galatians,
1535 (Chapters 1–4)* © 1963, 1991 Concordia Publishing
House. Used with permission. cph.org.

Luther's *The Freedom of a Christian* is reprinted from
*Luther's Works, Volume 31: Career of the Reformer I*
© 1957 Fortress Press. Used by permission.

Visit us online at www.fordhampress.com.

Library of Congress Control Number: 2022905135

Printed in the United States of America

24 23 22    5 4 3 2 1

First edition

# GRACE AND GRATITUDE

Past Light on Present Life:
Theology, Ethics, and Spirituality

*Roger Haight, SJ, Alfred Pach III,*
and *Amanda Avila Kaminski,* series editors

These volumes are offered to the academic community of teachers and learners in the fields of Christian history, theology, ethics, and spirituality. They introduce classic texts by authors whose contributions have markedly affected the development of Christianity, especially in the West. The texts are accompanied by an introductory essay on context and key themes and followed by an interpretation that dialogically engages the original message with the issues of ethics, theology, and spirituality in the present.

# Contents

I – Introduction to Luther and the Texts     I

II – The Texts: Martin Luther on Justification
    by Grace through Faith     19

Selection from Luther's
    *Lectures on Galatians* (1535)     21
Martin Luther: *The Freedom of a Christian*     74

III – Grace and Gratitude: Appropriating Luther's
    Spirituality Today     123

FURTHER READING     143

ABOUT THE SERIES     145

ABOUT THE EDITORS     151

# GRACE AND GRATITUDE

# I

## Introduction to Luther and the Texts

On a sultry day in July of the year 1505 a lonely traveler was trudging over a parched road on the outskirts of the Saxon village of Stotternheim. He was a young man, short but sturdy, and wore the dress of a university student. As he approached the village, the sky became overcast. Suddenly there was a shower, then a crashing storm. A bolt of lightning rived the gloom and knocked the man to the ground. Struggling to rise, he cried in terror, "St. Anne help me! I will become a monk."[1]

Thus did Roland Bainton introduce his biography of Luther seventy years ago, as if to remind the reader that what he wrought in Western history was set in motion by the meteorological accident of a lightning bolt. While more randomness than we like to imagine underlies all history, a lucid logic underpins Luther's theology, ethics, and spirituality. What makes him still more interesting lies in the way that these ordinarily quite distinct currents of thought intermingle with each other. It is difficult to determine where logical priority lies. That is no mean value.

Another reason makes Luther crucial for understanding Christian spirituality, and it too goes to the intrinsic character of his thinking. Reacting to what he deemed the effects of nominalist scholastic theology, Luther, as a scripture scholar, turned to scripture as the primary authority and point of departure for grounding his views. He was supported in this by the movement of renaissance scholarship. But Luther's appeal to scripture appeared as an alternative way of thinking to what was in place in the universities. He proposed at the opportune moment a "new" method of critical theology, one that bore a credibility that rived the theological world at the time in two. The two texts that follow represent Luther first as a biblical theologian drawing from the resources of scripture and then as explaining his position to the pope and his critics. But we begin by recalling salient factors in his formation.

## Martin Luther

Martin Luther was born in 1483 in northern Germany into a working-class family. However, Luther received an education, a bachelor of arts degree in 1502, and a Master of Arts in 1505, just before the incident of the summer storm. He was a religious man, and two weeks after the event he entered the Augustinian cloister in Erfurt. Two years later he was ordained a priest. Because he was gifted, Luther was assigned to study scripture and did some teaching. Over the winter of 1510–1511, he had an opportunity to visit Rome as a delegate of his monastery for a meeting on Augustinian affairs. At the end of that sojourn, he was transferred to Wittenberg where he became a doctor of theology in 1512 and began teaching full-time. In 1515, he lectured on *Romans*; in the fall of 1516, he began his series of lectures on *Galatians* for the first time. Early in 1517, already outspoken on the nature of theology, Luther posted theses attacking scholastic theology, and, in November of that year, he made public his ninety-five theses against indulgences. As these texts were passed around and became known, they caused the reaction that snowballed into the Reformation. Looking back from our secularized and pluralistic context, the magnitude of the events that followed seem as sudden and unlikely as a bolt of lightning. The church of Luther's youth was ripe for reform but no more than it had been in the two previous centuries, and everyone wanted it. The papacy during the last part of the fifteenth century was notorious in its lifestyle; clerical culture was corrupted top to bottom by systemic financial improprieties; theology had drifted away from popular Christianity into an abstract ideological world. These broad generalizations no doubt need to be qualified, but Erasmus exposed them through satire in his *In Praise of Folly*, which first appeared in 1511, and Luther encountered all of it up close. Luther learned about the papal court in his visit to Rome where the foundation stone for St. Peter's Basilica had been laid in 1506. He had read a scholastic theology that was radically different from the scripture he studied. Luther also had a scrupulous conscience in matters of personal sin that allowed him no peace in his relationship with God.[2] How did this relatively young theologian find the resources for what he finally effected?

One can postulate that Luther underwent at least two transformations in the course of the years from 1512 to 1518. The first consisted of an internalization of the world of the Bible. On the objective side, Luther as a theologian should be situated in the movement of Renaissance scholarship where understanding reaches for sources in past texts rather than the eternal truths of metaphysics. Scripture became an immediate source of God's revelation, bearing authoritative leverage over human construct. He was deeply affected by *Romans* and *Galatians*. The second transformation has been called Luther's "reformatory discovery" of the meaning of justification by grace through faith.[3] Commentators disagree on exactly when and how Luther came into full possession of this principle. Did he simply become convinced by Paul in *Romans* and *Galatians*? Martin Brecht believes that the depth and comprehensiveness of this conviction had to come through a lengthy process of reinforcement and cites textual evidence that it was solidified in 1518. It will become clear how deeply this theological principle reaches into Luther's life and thought. God's justice transcends and transforms any idea of a divine *quid pro quo*; it creates justice outside of itself by forgiveness and mercy. Luther found in this principle a modicum of peace and astonishing new energy.

Luther's life continued after 1518 at an extraordinary pace. He wrote *The Freedom of a Christian* in 1520, was excommunicated in 1521, but continued his leadership of the reform movement from his place in Wittenberg protected by the Elector of Saxony. He died in 1546.

## Luther on Galatians

We turn now to the first of the two selected texts representing Luther's spirituality.[4] The first, his commentary on Galatian, comes from his lectures in 1535, well after his conversion and fifteen years after the second text, his treatise on the Christian life. The later text still bears the power of the inner convictions that Paul's letter communicated to Luther earlier about the role of faith in contrast to reliance on law in the spiritual life. We begin by citing the scriptural text and then analyzing Luther's appropriation of it. A number of key words in or implied by the text help to lift up the inner logic of what Luther finds in Paul's lectures on Galatians: sin, justification, merit, law, works, faith, love, union with Christ, gratitude, freedom, and the contrast between the outer actions performed and the inner disposition of a person. All of these terms whirl around an interior contrast of intentions, between actively obeying the law to gain favor with God and a humble submission to the transforming power of God's grace accepting me as a sinner.[5]

15. We, who are Jews by nature and not sinners from among the Gentiles, 16. [yet] who know that a person is not justified by works of the law but through faith in Jesus Christ, even we have believed in Christ Jesus that we may be justified by faith in Christ and not by works of the law, because by works of the law no one will be justified. 17. But if, in seeking to be justified in Christ, we ourselves are found to be sinners, is Christ then a minister of sin? Of course not! 18. But if I am building up again those things that I tore down, then I show myself to be a transgressor. 19. For through the law I died to the law, that I might live for God. I have been crucified with Christ; 20. yet I live, no longer I, but Christ lives in me; insofar as I now live in the flesh, I live by faith in the Son of God who has loved me and given himself up for me. 21. I do not nullify the grace of God; for if justification comes through the law, then Christ died for nothing. (Galatians 2:15–20)

Luther's commentary on these verses of Galatians adds up to a short treatise on the basic principle of his spirituality: justification by grace through faith. Luther announces early on that he pitches the treatise against all ideas that human beings can merit any good standing before God on the basis of their natural power. Luther, with a strong doctrine of sin, completely rejects the ability of human beings to effect in any way their own salvation or any advance toward union with God. What follows synopsizes under three headings Luther's construal of the Pauline sources of Christian spirituality with the ideas of conversion, the effects of faith in the Christian life, and how this leads to what can be called a Christ mysticism. These ideas represent the basic principle of his spirituality in the dynamic terms of a process.

*Conversion.* Given the situation of sin that characterizes all human nature, Luther outlines the process of salvation, or human turning to God, in two steps. A person first comes to realize that the law, which commands human perfection, actually convicts the self of sin by mirroring back to consciousness the ideals to which one is called but never measures up. Then, out of a recognition of impotence relative to self-salvation, the person turns to the gospel and especially its messenger Christ. Christ bears the forgiveness of God that, by accepting persons as they are, as distinct from any idealized image or striving, transforms their being and their consciousness into persons embraced by God. Transforming faith, as Paul Tillich says, consists of accepting one's acceptance.

A condition for understanding how this process works lies in recognizing the character of faith that Luther presupposes. It is not an intellectual act of belief by which the mind decides that something is true. Luther does not view faith as an affirmation of propositions on the basis of an authoritative witness. Rather, faith involves a personal existential clinging that injects will and emotion into the dynamics of faith making it something akin to fundamental all-embracing trust.

*The effects of faith.* Christian faith aims primarily at Christ, and its effect is union with Christ. Given the order of the scriptural verses, Luther does not get there explicitly until he comments on Galatians 2:20. One becomes tied to Christ by the clinging of faith. Faith moves inside out; it is not self-reliant but looks outside the self to Christ, and does not turn back on itself. It does not examine or pay attention to the self. If it does, it immediately becomes anxious and turns to some form of self-reliance that distances a person from Christ. The symbol for this self-help in Luther is "works," which he correlates with law. By contrast, the righteousness effected by faith is not our own, but Christ's. Turning to Christ means not being confident in oneself but allowing Christ into one's life.

Several other results flow from faith's attachment to Christ and his revelation of God. One acquires a new freedom of conscience, which Luther describes as death to slavish attempts to obey the law and a transcendence of rule-based spirituality. Faith in Christ includes a certain being above the law and above the world. Law, sin, death, and evil can do one no harm. Christ is the Victor whose rule over all these elements prevents faithful persons from harm. "Therefore a Christian, properly defined, is free of all laws and is subject to nothing, internally or externally."[6] The Christian transcends the entire world. Christ constitutes them "as judges over all kinds of doctrine and [they] become lords over all the laws of the entire world."[7] Faith includes a confidence that makes Christians offspring and heirs of God, who, in hope, possess the promise of eternal life.

These new inner dispositions change human behavior. Faith repositions good works in the spiritual life. They do not establish union with God but flow from the union with God constituted by clinging to Christ. They do not cause justification but follow from faith that accepts the gift of justification. Faith results in the joy and gratitude of being accepted by God.

*Christ mysticism.* The idea of a "Christ mysticism" provides a way of summing up the spirituality contained in this short treatise. Union by faith's attachment to Christ sets up an abiding structure of Christian life that has an external and an internal or spiritual dimension. One lives simultaneously on two planes, in two relationships, that constitute a person's behavior. On the basis of flesh, in the sense of physical, empirical behavior, one takes part in earthly affairs "in such a way that there is no difference between [the Christian] and an ungodly man."[8] Everything seems the same, yet everything is different by the inner clinging of faith that mediates Christ living within a person. Law is associated with external behavior; grace and faith belong to inner spiritual life. Adhering to Christ becomes the inner, orienting, and, in the end, predominant force of a person's life. Some might hesitate to associate this union with Christ with some idea of mysticism. But the more one attends to Luther's language about the communication between

Christ and the person of faith, the more convincing the term "mysticism" becomes.

## Luther's *The Freedom of a Christian*

Luther's *The Freedom of a Christian* is a classic text. The relatively short essay summarized his conception of Christian spirituality when it had been truly internalized, and he strove to express it clearly and accurately. But it transcends the moment. The date of authorship was 1520, an extremely busy year for Luther. He was convinced, however, that he should communicate his views directly to the pope. The essay takes up many of the themes found in his commentary on Galatians and, in that respect, it is repetitious. But the shift of literary form and the way he arranged things give a fuller picture of his conception of the Christian life. The five subheadings used here simply highlight conceptions rather than represent the structure of the work. Luther's broad outline appears in these two sentences: "A Christian is a perfectly free lord of all, subject to none." "A Christian is a perfectly dutiful servant of all, subject to all."[9] The two statements capture Luther's propensity for polarity, tension, and paradox.

*The outer and the inner person.* Luther begins this work with an anthropological framework that governs the whole essay: "Man," he writes, "has a twofold nature, a spiritual and a bodily one."[10] He uses the spatial distinction between "inner" and "outer" to contrast the spiritual with the fleshly. The external side of human existence refers to the empirical and physical self and includes all the spontaneous emotional and biological tendencies that Paul refers to as temptation leading to sin. In contrast and tension with the physical and fleshly, subjectivity and intentionality reveal the domain of the human spirit and spirituality. The distinction of a spirituality of works and one of faith lines up with this duality. Given these two dimensions of the human, it is important to note what Luther intends when he points to "works, being inanimate things."[11] Luther is not exploring degrees of human subjectivity here. Everyone knows that human activity varies from being highly intentional to unthinking reaction. But he is pointing out the world of difference between intentional faith and mechanical behavior. The target is the idea that external devotions of themselves, as perfunctory actions, can earn God's favor.[12]

*Law and gospel.* The contrast between law and gospel also correlates with outer/inner and works/faith, but, in this work, Luther shows how the contrast opens up a deep structure of scripture itself. Scripture is divided into two parts: commandments and promises, or law and gospel. The law and commandments teach us to do good, and in this sense are themselves good; but they do not give or provide power. We cannot do what we ought to do. All are sinners, convicted by the law against coveting. The law thus pushes people into despair and a need for help because the law must be fulfilled. The other part of scripture is promise or gospel, given to those who believe. The law will be fulfilled only through Christ and may be appropriated only through faith that accepts Christ. Luther thus pushes the tension between law and gospel beyond the dynamics of personal life to provide a framework for understanding the entirety of salvation history. It becomes a basic worldview.

*The effects of grace.* Luther describes the effects of faith in somewhat more expansive terms in *Freedom* compared with Galatians. Faith, first of all, induces a freedom from the law; the Christian does not need works for justification and therefore technically no longer needs the law. Faith relies on the promise of God in Christ. Luther calls the second effect an absolute trust in God that acknowledges God's truthfulness. Absolute trust excludes doubt. In Aquinas, final salvation lies out front in a teleological structure of life leading to an end, which, due to human frailty, is always uncertain. In Luther, faith is existential, and faith itself carries its own certitude.

The third effect is union with Christ, as in the case of a bride and a bridegroom. Luther uses strikingly realistic imagery here. The effect of the union in this Christ mysticism entails a mutual communication of qualities: a wonderful exchange. The partners are equalized as in a marriage across social barriers. Christ assumes our sin, death, and damnation, and we share and possess his grace, life, and salvation.[13] Even more realistic is the physical image of radiant iron in the fire. "Just as the heated iron glows like fire because of the union of fire with it, so the Word imparts its qualities to the soul."[14]

*Priesthood of all believers.* This concept is drawn from the New Testament, but here Luther situates it as an entailment of his Christ mysticism. Christ is king and priest. As king, Christ rules sovereignly over spiritual and heavenly things; as priest, he intercedes for us in heaven and instructs us inwardly by his Spirit. These gifts are shared by the logic of the union of the Christian with Christ and the wonderful exchange. Therefore, all Christians are kings and priests. As kings, as explained earlier, Christians do not fear; they are above all things; lord of all by virtue of the spiritual power of Christ within, so that the Christian is free. As priests, all have power in faith to pray for others, to intercede for them, and to teach one another divine things. We are all fellow priests even though this does not mean that the power may be exercised publicly. Ministers and teachers require appointment by the community, but that is almost an "aside" compared with the inner dynamics of the spiritual life.

*An active spirituality.* Luther does not accept the critique that his conception of the life of faith is passive or quietist. The charge requires that he propose some positive function of human action, to law, and to human works. For this, he turns to the gospel image of the good tree bearing good fruit (Mt 7:18). This highlights the priority of faith relative to salvation and grace; good actions flow from an already justified person.[15] Further, law has positive functions in everyday life: it keeps the body or outer self under control, and, more positively, it functions to regulate society, the earthly kingdom. On this external level, works may be regarded as positive means for expressing love for one's neighbor. In this way Luther comes to the second of his initial propositions that the Christian is the servant of all. Faith is active through love that "finds expression in works of the freest service, cheerfully and lovingly done, with which a man willingly serves another without hope of reward" because he is already satisfied by the wealth of faith.[16]

We conclude, therefore, that a Christian lives not in himself but in Christ and in his neighbor. Otherwise he is not a Christian. He lives in Christ through faith, in his neighbor through love. By faith he is caught up beyond himself into God. By love he descends beneath himself into his neighbor. Yet he always remains in God and in God's love.[17]

## The Revolution that Luther Wrought

The classic language of Luther about justification by grace through faith is familiar to Lutherans and most mainline Protestants. But if they have not studied the Reformation, they may be less cognizant of the revolutionary character of what Luther proposed at the time. What follows supplements introduction to the texts with commentary on the important role these spiritual views of Luther had on people's understanding of Christianity and their efforts to live it. Noting how Luther's ideas affected his world assumes that by some analogy they may find resonances in the spiritual interests of our time.

*Revolution* and *reform* are slippery terms. But within the framework of the theology, ethics, and spirituality of late medieval Christianity, Luther's moves in relation to Scholasticism stand out by dramatic and explosive contrast. Luther sent Christian theology in the West in a new direction compared to thought in the high and late medieval periods. He represents a new way of thinking for that time, involving a different theological method, and the use of a language quite unlike that of Thomas Aquinas and the medieval universities. In some cases, the same words had different meanings or specific references that complicated communication. The point can be made without a detailed analysis of the topics in the schools of the fifteenth century; simply contrasting several features of Luther's language with that of Aquinas reveals different imaginative frameworks for understanding.[18] Four changes in supposition and method, proposed in terms of an implicit contrast, show that these texts, which may seem straightforward to Christians today, sprang from premises that forced people to reconsider some basics.

*From philosophy to the study of scripture.* Western theology learned the categories of Aristotle in the twelfth and thirteenth centuries, and it became the lingua franca of the scholastic theology of the late medieval period. Philosophical reasoning came to play a major role in forging an analytical method and an objective analogical form of understanding. The turn to scripture offered a fresh look at content and also principles that dictated either starting points or conclusions to be defended. In contrast to Scholasticism, Luther rode the crest of a wave of a Renaissance scholarship, a return to early sources that contained rich content. Translation, study, and reflection on the Bible was especially revelatory, because it frequently appeared to say things that history had gradually construed in different ways. Theology for Luther was biblical theology; its main method was commentary on scriptures. The readings show that what he taught in discursive form had its basis in the texts of scripture. This constituted a way of doing theology that, although not antithetical to objective analytical reflection, exemplified a way of thinking theologically that fundamentally differed from the Scholasticism in place.[19]

*From objective reasoning to existential encounter with Christ.* Whereas the christology of the schools talked about Christ on the basis of the traditional doctrines about Christ,

Luther's deepest imaginative framework consisted of an existential life-encounter with Christ. Luther did not think of faith as belief in the truth about Christ; he wrote out of a personal surrender to Christ, a decisive clinging to the person of Christ with trust and confidence. The meaning of assertions in Luther come from a different epistemological source when compared with university theology: on the one side, understanding based on objective analysis;[20] on the other, transforming existential faith experience. A good example of this is found in the theology of grace, that is, God's favor that constitutes a saving presence. In Augustine, grace referred most directly to the Holy Spirit, because the problem that bedeviled him concerned how a wounded soul weighed down by sin could open up to God. Aquinas maintained that tradition in a complex Aristotelian way. But in Luther the direct correlative of the term "grace" is Christ rather than God as Spirit. Jesus Christ is God's grace in Luther, and the primary theological analysis of this consists of his description of a conversion experience of turning to Christ.

*From an analogical imagination to a dialectical imagination.*[21] An analogical imagination penetrates differences among things to grasp elements of similitude or structural congruity. It rests on a relatively easy confidence in continuity between what we think and the way things are; it tends to find harmony between the worlds of God and human experience. God has supplied multiple bridges between Creator and creation. The dialectical imagination emphasizes the difference between God and human beings, God's world and ours, especially between God's will and human will, and it tends to think in oppositional terms. God interrupts and frequently appears "over against" human desires and performance. Fundamentally, for the religious imagination, human existence is not what it should be but is plagued by sin, and the distance between Creator and creatures is absolute and unbridgeable. Luther is an archetypal dialectical thinker, and this quality gives his thought a certain stark realism. Luther's theology should be understood in its first or initial perceptions as reflecting a reaction to serious problems, as contrast experiences of things gone wrong. As Tracy says, the languages of both analogy and dialectic are absolutely necessary to approximate the truth.[22]

*From the problem of finitude and death to the problem of sin and guilt.* The theology of grace has as its most elemental problem the Christian conception of the relationship between God and human beings. And some conception of grace always lies at the base of every Christian spirituality. A comparison of the theology of grace of Aquinas and Luther shows that the fundamental problem of human existence to which grace is an answer has changed with Luther. In Aquinas, the basic problem is the end of human existence; what happens to finite existence at death? What is the goal of human existence? The question invites a teleological perspective of reflection on human destiny. Grace empowers a new status and way of life enabling human existence to overcome death and arrive at its revealed supernatural goal. In Luther, the main problem is sin; we are stuck in it, not in the future but right now. Grace in Luther takes on the contours of divine forgiveness and a reconstituted personal relationship with God, negotiated by Jesus Christ, and clung to in this world by the grace continually made present to our faith in Christ. The theological point comes to focus in one's personal relationship with God now. The change is major, even though neither position excludes the other.

These four shifts help to show that something rather deep was going on in Luther's theology. The texts that follow outline the basic structure of his ethical thinking and the language of his spirituality and conception of the Christian life. They had an impact on many in Europe during the sixteenth century. The texts are classic because they represent an inner logic that has consistently rung true to Christian encounter with the world and with God. The question is whether and how these polarities also correlate with experience in our secular and pragmatic societies.

## Notes

1. Roland H. Bainton, *Here I Stand: A Life of Martin Luther* (Nashville and New York: Abingdon Press, 1950), 21.

2. Scott Hendrix, *Martin Luther: Visionary Reformer* (New Haven and London: Yale University Press, 2015), 37.

3. This is described by Martin Brecht, *Martin Luther, I–III* (Philadelphia: Fortress Press, 1985–93), at I, 221–37.

4. These texts could be classified as biblical exegesis and theological reflection. But this volume aims at a deeper framework where Luther's imagination conceives the basic structure of spiritual life.

5. Recall that the point here is not to explain Luther's text, helped by endless secondary sources, but to open up a space to its being read today as bearing meaning.

6. Martin Luther, *Luther's Works, 26, Lectures on Galatians 1535*, ed. Jaroslav Pelikan (Saint Louis: Concordia Publishing House,1963), 134.

7. Luther, *Galatians, 134.*

8. Luther, *Galatians, 171.*

9. Martin Luther, *The Freedom of a Christian,* in *Luther's Works, 31, The Career of the Reformer: I* (Philadelphia: Muhlenberg Press: 1963), 344.

10. Luther, Freedom, 344.

11. Luther, *Freedom,* 353.

12. The principle is general, but it would not be wrong to see it represented by the selling and buying of indulgences.

13. Luther, *Freedom,* 351–53.

14. Luther, *Freedom,* 349.

15. Luther, *Freedom,* 361. The metaphor preserves several points in Luther's teaching: a) the priority of faith; b) grace comes as pure mercy, through Christ and his Word, received in faith; c) salvation is all at once; no need of works, one enters into a vertical saved relationship to God, now, not teleologically by works into a saved

future; d) freedom by grace from law, obligations, works; e) salvation that does not transpire through actions; actions only display the salvation that is there already constituted by faith.

16. Luther, *Freedom*, 365.

17. Luther, Freedom, 371.

18. The volume entitled *The Medieval Structure of Spirituality* of this series is dedicated to several key texts from Aquinas's *Summa Theologiae*. His method of theology appropriated the discovery of Aristotle and addressed the emergent universities in Europe; it can serve as an implicit background for describing the revolutionary character of Luther's initiatives. The contrast does not intend a critique of Aquinas or the Scholasticism Luther was taught but underlines the significant difference between methods and ways of thinking. See Roger Haight, *The Experience and Language of Grace* (Mahwah, NJ: Paulist Press, 1979), chaps. 3–4.

19. A figure like Erasmus of Rotterdam (1466–36) and others show that Luther was not a pioneer here but he left a strong and distinctive mark.

20. This is not meant to suggest that objective analysis lacks religious experience behind it.

21. These categories of an "analogical imagination" and a "dialectical imagination" are drawn from David Tracy, *The Analogical Imagination: Christian Theology and the Culture of Pluralism* (New York: Crossroad, 1981), 405–21. Types are meant to illuminate and provide openings for discussion rather than to pigeonhole theologians or methods.

22. Tracy, *Analogical*, 421.

# II
## The Texts

# Selection from Luther's
## *Lectures on Galatians* (1535)

16. *Yet who know that a man is not justified by works of the Law but through faith in Jesus Christ.*

These words, "works of the Law," are to be taken in the broadest possible sense and are very emphatic. I am saying this because of the smug and idle scholastics and monks, who obscure such words in Paul—in fact, everything in Paul—with their foolish and wicked glosses, which even they themselves do not understand. Therefore take "works of the Law" generally, to mean whatever is opposed to grace: Whatever is not grace is Law, whether it be the Civil Law, the Ceremonial Law, or the Decalog. Therefore even if you were to do the work of the Law, according to the commandment, "You shall love the Lord your God with all your heart, etc." (Matt. 22:37), you still would not be justified in the sight of God; for a man is not justified in the sight of God; for a man is not justified by works of the Law. But more detail on this later on.

Thus for Paul "works of the Law" means the works of the entire Law. Therefore one should not make a distinction between the Decalog and ceremonial laws. Now if the work of the Decalog does not justify, much less will circumcision, which is a work of the Ceremonial Law. When Paul says, as he often does, that a man is not justified by the Law or by the works of the Law, which means the same thing in Paul, he is speaking in general about the entire Law; he is contrasting the righteousness of faith with the righteousness of the entire Law, with everything that can be done on the basis of the Law, whether by divine power or by human.[1] For by the righteousness of the Law, he says, a man is not pronounced righteous in the sight of God; but God imputes the righteousness of faith freely through His mercy, for the sake of Christ. It is, therefore, with a certain emphasis and vehemence that he said "by works of the Law." For there is no doubt that the Law is holy, righteous, and good; therefore the works of the Law are holy, righteous, and good. Nevertheless, a man is not justified in the sight of God through them.

Hence the opinion of Jerome and others is to be rejected when they imagine that here Paul is speaking about the works of the Ceremonial Law, not about those of the Decalog.[2] If I concede this, I am forced to concede also that the Ceremonial Law was good and holy. Surely circumcision and other laws about rites and about the temple were righteous and holy, for they were commanded by God as much as the moral laws were. But then they say: "But after Christ the ceremonial laws were fatal." They invent this out of their own heads, for it does not appear anywhere in Scripture. Besides, Paul is not speaking here about the Gentiles, for whom the ceremonies would be fatal, but about the Jews, for whom they were good; indeed, he himself observed them. Thus even at the time when the ceremonial laws were holy, righteous, and good, they were not able to justify.

Therefore Paul is speaking not only about a part of the Law, which is also good and holy, but about the entire Law. He means that a work done in accordance with the entire Law does not justify. Nor is he speaking about a sin against the Law or a deed of the flesh, but about "the work of the Law," that is, a work performed in accordance with the Law.

Therefore refraining from murder or adultery—whether this is done by natural powers or by human strength or by free will or by the gift and power of God—still does not justify. But the works of the Law can be performed either before justification or after justification. Before justification many good men even among the pagans—such as Xenophon, Aristides, Fabius, Cicero, Pomponius Atticus, etc.—performed the works of the Law and accomplished great things.[3] Cicero suffered death courageously in a righteous and good cause. Pomponius was a man of integrity and veracity; for he himself never lied, and he could not bear it if others did. Integrity and veracity are, of course, very fine virtues and very beautiful works of the Law; but these men were not justified by these works. After justification, moreover, Peter, Paul, and all other Christians have done and still do the works of the Law; but they are not justified by them either. "I am not aware of anything against myself," says Paul; that is, "No man can accuse me, but I am not thereby justified" (1 Cor. 4:4). Thus we see that Paul is speaking about the entire Law and all its works, not about sins against the Law.

Therefore the dangerous and wicked opinion of the papists is to be condemned. They attribute the merit of grace and the forgiveness of sins to the mere performance of the work. For they say that a good work performed before grace can earn a "merit of congruity"; but once grace has been obtained, the work that follows deserves eternal life by the "merit of condignity."[4] If a man outside a state of grace and in mortal sin performs a good work by his own natural inclination—such as reading or hearing Mass, giving alms, etc.—this man deserves grace "by congruity." Once he has obtained grace this way, he goes on to perform a work that merits eternal life "by condignity." Now in the first case God is not indebted to anyone. But because He is good and righteous, it is proper for Him to approve such a good work, even though it is performed in mortal sin, and to grant grace for such a deed. But once grace has been obtained, God has become a debtor and is obliged by right to grant eternal life. For now this is not only a work of the free will, carried out externally; but it is performed in the grace that makes a man pleasing before God, that is, in love.

Such is the theology of the antichristian kingdom. I am recounting it here to make Paul's argument more intelligible; for when two opposites are placed side by side, they become more evident. In addition, I want everyone to see how far these "blind guides of the blind" (Matt. 15:14) have strayed. By this wicked and blasphemous teaching they have not only obscured the Gospel but have removed it altogether and have buried Christ completely. For if in a state of mortal sin I can do any tiny work that is not only pleasing before God externally and of itself but can even deserve grace "by congruity"; and if, once I have received grace, I am able to perform works according to grace, that is, according to love, and receive eternal life by a right—then what need do I have of the grace of God, the forgiveness of sins, the promise, and the death and victory of Christ? Then Christ has become altogether useless to me; for I have free will and the power to perform good works, and through this I merit grace "by congruity" and eventually eternal life "by condignity."

Such dreadful monstrosities and horrible blasphemies ought to be propounded to Turks and Jews, not to the church of Christ. This whole business clearly shows that the pope with his bishops, theologians, monks, and all the rest has neither knowledge nor concern about sacred things; nor do they care anything about the health of the flock, which is so deserted and so miserably scattered. For if they had seen, though only through a cloud, what Paul calls sin and what he calls grace, they would not have imposed such abominations and wicked lies on Christian people. They take mortal sin to be only the external work committed against the Law, such as murder, adultery, theft, etc. They did not see that ignorance, hatred, and contempt of God in the heart, ingratitude, murmuring against God, and resistance to the will of God are also mortal sin, and that the flesh cannot think, say, or do anything except what is diabolical and opposed to God. If they had seen that these huge plagues are rooted in the nature of man, they would not have dreamt so wickedly about the "merit of congruity" and the "merit of condignity."

Therefore there must be a proper and clear definition of what a wicked man or mortal sinner is. He is a holy hypocrite and murderer, as Paul was when he went to Damascus to persecute Jesus of Nazareth, to abolish the doctrine of Christ, to murder the faithful, and to overthrow the church of Christ altogether. Those were certainly extremely great and horrible sins against God, but Paul was unable to recognize them as such. For he was so completely blinded by a wicked zeal for God that he regarded these unspeakable crimes of his as the height of righteousness and an act of worship and obedience most pleasing to God. Can such saints, who defend such horrible sins as the height of righteousness, be supposed to merit grace?

With Paul, therefore, we totally deny the "merit of congruity" and the "merit of condignity"; and with complete confidence we declare that these speculations are merely the tricks of Satan, which have never been performed or demonstrated by any examples. For God has never given anyone grace and eternal life for the merit of congruity or the merit of condignity. Therefore these disputations of the scholastics about merit of congruity and of condignity are nothing but empty fictions, the dreams of idle men; and yet the entire papacy is founded on these nonexistent things and depends on them to this day. For every monk imagines as follows to himself: "By the observance of my holy rule I am able to merit grace 'by congruity.' And by the works I perform after receiving this grace I am able to accumulate such a treasure of merit that it will not only be enough for me to obtain eternal life but can also be given or sold to others." This is how all the monks have taught and lived. In defense of this horrible blasphemy against Christ there is nothing that the papists will not attempt against us today. Among them all, the more holy and self-righteous a hypocrite is, the more vicious an enemy he is of the Gospel of Christ.

Now the true meaning of Christianity is this: that a man first acknowledge, through the Law, that he is a sinner, for whom it is impossible to perform any good work. For the Law says: "You are an evil tree. Therefore everything you think, speak, or do is opposed to God. Hence you cannot deserve grace by your works. But if you try to do so, you make the bad even worse; for since you are an evil tree, you cannot produce anything except evil fruits, that is, sins. 'For whatever does not proceed from faith is sin' (Rom. 14:23)." Trying to merit grace by preceding works, therefore, is trying to placate God with sins, which is nothing but heaping sins upon sins, making fun of God, and provoking His wrath. When a man is taught this way by the Law, he is frightened and humbled. Then he really sees the greatness of his sin and finds in himself not one spark of the love of God; thus he justifies God in His Word and confesses that he deserves death and eternal damnation. Thus the first step in Christianity is the preaching of repentance and the knowledge of oneself.

The second step is this: If you want to be saved, your salvation does not come by works; but God has sent His only Son into the world that we might live through Him. He was crucified and died for you and bore your sins in His own body (1 Peter 2:24). Here there is no "congruity" or work performed before grace, but only wrath, sin, terror, and death. Therefore the Law only shows sin, terrifies, and humbles; thus it prepares us for justification and drives us to Christ. For by His Word God has revealed to us that He wants to be a merciful Father to us. Without our merit—since, after all, we cannot merit anything—He wants to give us forgiveness of sins, righteousness, and eternal life for the sake of Christ. For God is He who dispenses His gifts freely to all,[5] and this is the praise of His deity. But He cannot defend this deity of His against the self-righteous people who are unwilling to accept grace and eternal life from Him freely but want to earn it by their own works. They simply want to rob Him of the glory of His deity. In order to retain it, He is compelled to send forth His Law, to terrify and crush those very hard rocks as though it were thunder and lightning.

This, in summary, is our theology about Christian righteousness, in opposition to the abominations and monstrosities of the sophists about "merit of congruity and of condignity" or about works before grace and after grace. Smug people, who have never struggled with any temptations or true terrors of sin and death, were the ones who made up these empty dreams out of their own heads; therefore they do not understand what they are saying or what they are talking about, for they cannot supply any examples of such works done either before grace or after grace. Therefore these are useless fables, with which the papists delude both themselves and others.

The reason is that Paul expressly states here that a man is not justified by the deeds of the Law, whether they are those that precede (of which he is speaking here) or those that follow justification. Thus you see that Christian righteousness is not an "inherent form," as they call it.[6] For they say: When a man does a good work, God accepts it; and for this work He infuses charity into him. This infused charity, they say, is a quality that is attached to the heart; they call it "formal righteousness." (It is a good idea for you to know this manner of speaking.) Nothing is more intolerable to them than to be told that this quality, which informs the heart as whiteness does a wall, is not righteousness. They cannot climb any higher than this cogitation of human reason: Man is righteous by means of his formal righteousness, which is grace making him pleasing before God, that is, love.[7] Thus they attribute formal righteousness to an attitude and "form" inherent in the soul, namely, to love, which is a work and gift according to the Law; for the Law says: "You shall love the Lord" (Matt. 22:37). And they say that this righteousness is worthy of eternal life; that he who has it is "formally righteous"; and, finally, that he is righteous in fact, because he is now performing good works, for which eternal life is due him. This is the opinion of the sophists—and of the best among them at that.

Others are not even that good, such as Scotus and Occam.[8] They said that this love which is given by God is not necessary to obtain the grace of God, but that even by his own natural powers a man is able to produce a love for God above all things. Scotus disputes this way: "If a man can love a creature, a young man love a girl, or a covetous man love money—all of which are a lesser good—he can also love God, who is a greater good. If by his natural powers he has a love for the creature, much more does he have a love for the Creator." This argument left all the sophists confounded, and none of them could refute it. Nevertheless, this is what they said:[9]

"Scripture requires us to say that in addition to our natural love, with which He is not satisfied, God also demands a love that He Himself grants." Thus they accuse God of being a severe tyrant and a cruel taskmaster, who is not content that I observe and fulfill His Law but demands also that beyond the Law, which I can easily fulfill, I dress up my obedience with additional qualities and adornments. It is as though the lady of the house were not content that her cook had prepared the food very well but scolded her for not wearing precious garments and adorning herself with a golden crown while she prepared the food. What sort of housewife would that be who, after her cook has done everything she is required to do and has done it superbly, would demand that she should also wear a golden crown, which it is impossible for her to have? Likewise, what sort of God would that be who would demand that we fulfill His Law, which we otherwise observe by our natural powers, with an ornamentation that we cannot possess?

To avoid the impression of contradicting themselves, they make a distinction at this point and say that the Law can be fulfilled in two ways: first, according to the content of the act; secondly, according to the intention of Him who gave the commandment.[10] According to the content of the act, that is, so far as the deed itself is concerned, we can simply fulfill everything that the Law commands. But we cannot do so according to the intention of Him who gave the commandment; for this means that God is not content that you have performed and fulfilled everything commanded in the Law (although He has no more than this to demand of you), but He requires in addition that you keep the Law in love—not the natural love that you have but a supernatural and divine love that He Himself confers. What is this but to make God a tyrant and a tormentor who demands of us what we cannot produce? In a sense it is as though they were saying that if we are damned, the fault is not so much in us as in God, who requires us to keep His Law in this fashion.

I am reciting all this to make you see how far they have strayed from the meaning of Scripture with their declaration that by our own natural powers we are able to love God above all things, or at least that by the mere performance of the deed we are able to merit grace and eternal life. And because God is not content if we fulfill the Law according to the content of the act but also wants us to fulfill it according to the intention of Him who gave the commandment, therefore Sacred Scripture requires us to have a supernatural quality infused into us from heaven, namely, love, which they call the formal righteousness that informs and adorns faith and makes it justify us. Thus faith is the body, the shell, or the color; but love is the life, the kernel, or the form.

Such are the dreams of the scholastics. But where they speak of love, we speak of faith. And while they say that faith is the mere outline[11] but love is its living colors and completion, we say in opposition that faith takes hold of Christ and that He is the form that adorns and informs faith as color does the wall. Therefore Christian faith is not an idle quality or an empty husk in the heart, which may exist in a state of mortal sin until love comes along to make it alive. But if it is true faith, it is a sure trust and firm acceptance in the heart.

It takes hold of Christ in such a way that Christ is the object
of faith, or rather not the object but, so to speak, the One
who is present in the faith itself. Thus faith is a sort of knowledge or darkness that nothing can see. Yet the Christ of whom
faith takes hold is sitting in this darkness as God sat in the
midst of darkness on Sinai and in the temple.[12] Therefore our
"formal righteousness" is not a love that informs faith; but it
is faith itself, a cloud in our hearts, that is, trust in a thing we
do not see, in Christ, who is present especially when He cannot
be seen.

Therefore faith justifies because it takes hold of and possesses this treasure, the present Christ. But how He is present—this is beyond our thought; for there is darkness, as I
have said. Where the confidence of the heart is present, therefore, there Christ is present, in that very cloud and faith. This
is the formal righteousness on account of which a man is
justified; it is not on account of love, as the sophists say. In
short, just as the sophists say that love forms and trains faith,
so we say that it is Christ who forms and trains faith or who
is the form of faith. Therefore the Christ who is grasped by
faith and who lives in the heart is the true Christian righteousness, on account of which God counts us righteous and grants
us eternal life. Here there is no work of the Law, no love; but
there is an entirely different kind of righteousness, a new
world above and beyond the Law. For Christ or faith is neither
the Law nor the work of the Law. But we intend later on to
go into more detail on this issue, which the sophists have
neither understood nor written about. For the present let it
be enough for us to have shown that Paul is speaking here
not only about the Ceremonial Law but about the entire Law.

I have warned in passing of the dangerous error of the
scholastic theologians, who taught that a man obtains forgiveness of sins and justification in the following manner: By
his works that precede grace, which they call a "merit of
congruity," he merits grace, which, according to them, is a
quality that inheres in the will, granted by God over and above

the love we have by our natural powers. They say that when a man has this quality, he is formally righteous and a true Christian. I say that this is a wicked and dangerous notion, which does not make a man a Christian but makes him a Turk, a Jew, an Anabaptist, or a fanatic. For who cannot perform a good work by his own powers without grace and thus merit grace? In this way these dreamers have made faith an empty quality in the soul, which is of no use alone, without love, but becomes effective and justifies when love is added to it.

They go on to say that the works that follow have the power to merit eternal life "by condignity," because God accepts the work that follows and applies it to eternal life, on account of the love that He has infused into man's will. Thus they say that God "accepts" a good work for eternal life but "disaccepts" an evil work for damnation and eternal punishment.[13] They have heard something in a dream about "acceptance" and have ascribed this relation to works. All this is false and blasphemous against Christ. Nevertheless, they do not all speak even this well; but some, as we have said, have taught that by our purely natural powers[14] we are able to love God above all things. These things are useful to know, to make Paul's argument clearer.

In opposition to these trifles and empty dreams, as we have noted briefly above, we teach faith and the true meaning of Christianity. First, a man must be taught by the Law to know himself, so that he may learn to sing: "All have sinned and fall short of the glory of God" (Rom. 3:23); again: "None is righteous, no, not one; no one understands, no one seeks for God. All have turned aside" (Rom. 3:10–12); again: "Against Thee only have I sinned" (Ps. 51:4). By this opposition of ours we drive men away from the merit of congruity and of condignity. Now once a man has thus been humbled by the Law and brought to the knowledge of himself, then he becomes truly repentant; for true repentance begins with fear and with the judgment of God. He sees that he is such a great sinner that he cannot find any means to be delivered from his sin by his own strength, effort, or works. Then he understands correctly what Paul means when he says that man is the slave and captive of sin, that God has consigned all men to sin, and that the whole world is guilty in the sight of God.[15] Then he sees that the doctrine of the sophists about the merit of congruity and of condignity is mere μσταιολογία (1 Tim. 1:6) and that the entire papacy is undermined.

Now he begins to sigh: "Then who can come to my aid?" Terrified by the Law, he despairs of his own strength; he looks about and sighs for the help of the Mediator and Savior. Then there comes, at the appropriate time, the saving Word of the Gospel, which says: "Take heart, my son; your sins are forgiven (Matt. 9:2). Believe in Jesus Christ, who was crucified for your sins. If you feel your sins, do not consider them in yourself but remember that they have been transferred to Christ, 'with whose stripes you are healed' (Is. 53:3)."

This is the beginning of salvation. By this means we are delivered from sin and justified, and eternal life is granted to us, not for our own merits and works but for our faith, by which we take hold of Christ. Therefore we, too, acknowledge a quality and a formal righteousness in the heart; but we do not mean love, as the sophists do, but faith, because the heart must behold and grasp nothing but Christ the Savior. Here it is necessary to know the true definition of Christ. Ignoring this altogether, the sophists have made Him a judge and a torturer, and have invented this stupid notion about the merit of congruity and of condignity.

But by the true definition Christ is not a lawgiver; He is a Propitiator and a Savior. Faith takes hold of this and believes without doubting that He has performed a superabundance of works and merits of congruity and condignity. He might have made satisfaction for all the sins of the world with only one drop of His blood,[16] but now He has made abundant satisfaction. Heb. 9:12: "With His own blood He entered once for all into the Holy Place." And Rom. 3:24–25: "Justified by His grace as a gift, through the redemption which is in

Christ Jesus, whom God put forward as an expiation by His blood." Therefore it is something great to take hold, by faith, of Christ, who bears the sins of the world (John 1:29). And this faith alone is counted for righteousness (Rom. 3–4).

Here it is to be noted that these three things are joined together: faith, Christ, and acceptance or imputation. Faith takes hold of Christ and has Him present, enclosing Him as the ring encloses the gem. And whoever is found having this faith in the Christ who is grasped in the heart, him God accounts as righteous. This is the means and the merit by which we obtain the forgiveness of sins and righteousness. "Because you believe in Me," God says, "and your faith takes hold of Christ, whom I have freely given to you as your Justifier and Savior, therefore be righteous." Thus God accepts you or accounts you righteous only on account of Christ, in whom you believe.

Now acceptance or imputation is extremely necessary, first, because we are not yet purely righteous, but sin is still clinging to our flesh during this life. God cleanses this remnant of sin in our flesh. In addition, we are sometimes forsaken by the Holy Spirit, and we fall into sins, as did Peter, David, and other saints. Nevertheless, we always have recourse to this doctrine, that our sins are covered and that God does not want to hold us accountable for them (Rom. 4). This does not mean that there is no sin in us, as the sophists have taught when they said that we must go on doing good until we are to longer conscious of any sin; but sin is always present, and the godly feel it. But it is ignored and hidden in the sight of God, because Christ the Mediator stands between; because we take hold of Him by faith, all our sins are sins no longer. But where Christ and faith are not present, here there is no forgiveness of sins or hiding of sins. On the contrary, here there is the sheer imputation and condemnation of sins. Thus God wants to glorify His Son, and He Himself wants to be glorified in us through Him.

When we have taught faith in Christ this way, then we also teach about good works. Because you have taken hold of

Christ by faith, through whom you are righteous, you should now go and love God and your neighbor. Call upon God, give thanks to Him, preach Him, praise Him, confess Him. Do good to your neighbor, and serve him; do your duty. These are truly good works, which flow from this faith and joy conceived in the heart because we have the forgiveness of sins freely through Christ.

Then whatever there is of cross or suffering to be borne later on is easily sustained. For the yoke that Christ lays upon us is sweet, and His burden is light (Matt. 11:30). When sin has been forgiven and the conscience has been liberated from the burden and the sting of sin, then a Christian can bear everything easily. Because everything within is sweet and pleasant, he willingly does and suffers everything. But when a man goes along in his own righteousness, then whatever he does and suffers is painful and tedious for him, because he is doing it unwillingly.

Therefore we define a Christian as follows: A Christian is not someone who has no sin or feels no sin; he is someone to whom, because of his faith in Christ, God does not impute his sin. This doctrine brings firm consolation to troubled consciences amid genuine terrors. It is not in vain, therefore, that so often and so diligently we inculcate the doctrine of the forgiveness of sins and of the imputation of righteousness for the sake of Christ, as well as the doctrine that a Christian does not have anything to do with the Law and sin, especially in a time of temptation. For to the extent that he is a Christian, he is above the Law and sin, because in his heart he has Christ, the Lord of the Law, as a ring has a gem. Therefore when the Law accuses and sin troubles, he looks to Christ; and when he has taken hold of Him by faith, he has present with him the Victor over the Law, sin, death, and the devil—the Victor whose rule over all these prevents them from harming him.

Therefore a Christian, properly defined, is free of all laws and is subject to nothing, internally or externally. But I purposely said, "To the extent that he is a Christian" (not "to the

extent that he is a man or a woman"); that is, to the extent
that he has his conscience trained, adorned, and enriched by
this faith, this great and inestimable treasure, or, as Paul calls
it, "this inexpressible gift" (2 Cor. 9:15), which cannot be
exalted and praised enough, since it makes men sons and heirs
of God. Thus a Christian is greater than the entire world. For
in his heart he has this seemingly small gift; yet the smallness
of this gift and treasure, which he holds in faith, is greater than
heaven and earth, because Christ, who is this gift, is greater.

When this doctrine, which pacifies consciences, remains
pure and intact, Christians are constituted as judges over all
kinds of doctrine and become lords over all the laws of the
entire world. Then they can freely judge that the Turk with
his Koran is damned, because he does not follow the right
way; that is, he does not acknowledge that he is a miserable
and damned sinner, and he does not take hold of Christ by
faith, for whose sake he could believe that his sins are forgiven. With similar confidence they can pronounce sentence
against the pope. He is damned with all his kingdom, because
he, with all his monks and universities, acts as though we
came to grace through the merit of congruity and as though
we were then received into heaven by the merit of condignity.
Here the Christian says: "That is not the right way to justify.
This is not the road to the stars.[17] For through my works
preceding grace I cannot merit grace by congruity, nor can I
deserve eternal life by condignity through my merits following
grace; but sin is forgiven and righteousness is imputed to him
who believes in Christ. This confidence makes him a son and
heir of God, who in hope possesses the promise of eternal
life. Through faith in Christ, therefore, and not through the
merit of congruity and of condignity, everything is granted
to us—grace, peace, the forgiveness of sins, salvation, and
eternal life."

Therefore this doctrine of the sententiaries about the merit
of congruity and condignity—with all their ceremonies, Masses,
and innumerable foundations of the papal kingdom—is an

abominable blasphemy against God, a sacrilege, and a denial
of Christ. Peter predicted it in these words from 2 Peter 2:1:
"There will be false teachers among you, who will secretly
bring in destructive heresies, even denying the Master who
bought them." It is as though he were saying: "The Master has
redeemed and bought us with His blood, to justify and save
us; this is the way of righteousness and salvation. But false
teachers will come; they will deny the Master and will blaspheme the way of truth, righteousness, and salvation. They will
invent new ways of falsehood and perdition, and many will
follow their perdition." Throughout this chapter Peter draws
an outstanding portrait of the papacy, which has neglected the
Gospel and faith in Christ and has taught human works and
traditions, like the merit of congruity and of condignity, special
days, foods, as well as persons, vows, the invocation of saints,
pilgrimages, purgatory, etc. The papists have imbibed these
fanatical opinions about traditions and works to such an extent
that it is impossible for them to understand a single syllable
about the Gospel, about faith, or about Christ.

This is sufficiently evident from the matter at hand. For
they usurp for themselves the right that belongs to Christ
alone. Only He delivers from sin and grants righteousness
and eternal life; yet they claim that they are able to obtain
these things by their own merits of congruity and of condignity, to the exclusion of Christ. Peter and the other apostles
call this bringing in "destructive heresies," denying Christ,
treading His blood underfoot, and blaspheming the Holy
Spirit and the grace of God. Therefore no one sees sufficiently
how horrible the idolatry of the papists is. As inestimable as
the gift offered to us in Christ is, that is how abominable these
papistic profanations are. Therefore they should not be lightly
dismissed or consigned to oblivion but should be diligently
considered. And this, by contrast, serves to magnify the grace
of God and the blessings of Christ. For the more I recognize
the profanation of the papistic Mass, the more I abhor and
detest it. The pope has taken away the true use of the Mass

and has simply turned it into merchandise that one may buy for the benefit of another person. There stood the Mass priest at the altar, an apostate who denied Christ and blasphemed the Holy Spirit; and he was doing a work not only for himself but for others, both living and dead, even for the entire church, and that simply by the mere performance of the act.

Even from this, therefore, it is evident that the patience of God is inestimable, since He did not destroy the whole papacy long ago and consume it with fire and brimstone, as he did Sodom and Gomorrah. But now these fine people want to cover and adorn their wickedness and infamy. For us this is intolerable. From the darkness and night of their hypocrisy we must drag them into the light, in order that the doctrine of justification, like the sun, may reveal their infamy and shame. This is why we gladly give sharp expression to the righteousness of faith—in order that the papists and all the sectarians may be confounded and this doctrine may be established and made certain in our hearts. And this is extremely necessary; for once we have lost this sun, we relapse into our former darkness. And it is horrendous to the highest degree that the pope should have managed to accomplish this in the church, that Christ should be denied, trodden underfoot, spit upon, and blasphemed—and all this by means of the Gospel and the sacraments, which the pope has so obscured and distorted that he has made them serve him against Christ in establishing and supporting his diabolical abominations. What darkness! And how infinite is the wrath of God!

*Even we have believed in Christ Jesus, in order to be justified by faith in Christ, and not by works of the Law.*

This is the true meaning of Christianity, that we are justified by faith in Christ, not by the works of the Law. Do not let yourself be swayed here by the wicked gloss of the sophists, who say that faith justifies only when love and good works are added to it. With this pernicious gloss they have darkened and distorted some of the finest texts of this sort. When a man hears that he should believe in Christ, but that faith does not justify unless this "form," that is, love, is added, then he quickly falls from faith and thinks to himself: "If faith does not justify without love, then faith is vain and useless, and love alone justifies; or unless faith is formed and adorned by love, it is nothing."

In support of this wicked and destructive gloss the opponents cite this passage from 1 Cor. 13:1–2: "If I speak in the tongues of men and of angels, and if I have prophetic powers and understand all mysteries and all knowledge, and if I have all faith, so as to remove mountains, but have not love, I am nothing."[18] They suppose that this passage is their wall of bronze. But they are men without understanding, and therefore they cannot grasp or see anything in Paul. With this false interpretation they have not only done injury to Paul's words but have also denied Christ and buried all His blessings. Therefore this gloss is to be avoided as a hellish poison, and we must conclude with Paul: By faith alone, not by faith formed by love, are we justified. We must not attribute the power of justifying to a "form" that makes a man pleasing to God; we must attribute it to faith, which takes hold of Christ the Savior Himself and possesses Him in the heart. This faith justifies without love and before love.

We concede that good works and love must also be taught; but this must be in its proper time and place, that is, when the question has to do with works, apart from this chief doctrine. But here the point at issue is how we are justified and attain eternal life. To this we answer with Paul: We are pronounced righteous solely by faith in Christ, not by the works of the Law or by love. This is not because we reject works or love, as our adversaries accuse us of doing, but because we refuse to let ourselves be distracted from the principal point at issue here, as Satan is trying to do. So since we are now dealing with the topic of justification, we reject and condemn works; for this topic will not allow of any discussion of good works. On this issue, therefore, we simply cut off all laws and all works of the Law.

"But the Law is good, righteous, and holy." Very well! But when we are involved in a discussion of justification, there is no room for speaking about the Law. The question is what Christ is and what blessing He has brought us. Christ is not the Law; He is not my work or that of the Law; He is not my love or that of the Law; He is not my chastity, obedience, or poverty. But He is the Lord of life and death, the Mediator and Savior of sinners, the Redeemer of those who are under the Law. By faith we are in Him, and He is in us (John 6:56). This Bridegroom, Christ, must be alone with His bride in His private chamber, and all the family and household must be shunted away. But later on, when the Bridegroom opens the door and comes out, then let the servants return to take care of them and serve them food and drink. Then let works and love begin.

Thus we must learn to distinguish all laws, even those of God, and all works from faith and from Christ, if we are to define Christ accurately. Christ is not the Law, and therefore He is not a task-master for the Law and for works; but He is the Lamb of God, who takes away the sin of the world (John 1:29). This is grasped by faith alone, not by love, which nevertheless must follow faith as a kind of gratitude. Therefore victory over sin and death, salvation, and eternal life do not come by the Law or by the deeds of the Law or by our will but by Jesus Christ alone. Hence faith alone justifies when it takes hold of this, as becomes evident from a sufficient division and induction:[19] Victory over sin and death does not come by the works of the Law or by our will; therefore it comes by Jesus Christ alone. Here we are perfectly willing to have ourselves called "solafideists"[20] by our opponents, who do not understand anything of Paul's argument. You who are to be the consolers of consciences that are afflicted, should teach this doctrine diligently, study it continually, and defend it vigorously against the abominations of the papists, Jews, Turks, and all the rest.[21]

*In order to be justified by faith in Christ, and not by works of the Law.*

All these words are to be read with feeling and emphasis. As I have warned before, Paul is speaking here not about the Ceremonial Law alone but about the entire Law. For the Ceremonial Law was as much the divine Law as the moral laws were. Thus circumcision, the institution of the priesthood, the service of worship, and the rituals were commanded by God as much as the Decalog was. In addition, it was the Law when Abraham was commanded to sacrifice his son Isaac. This work of Abraham pleased God as much as other ceremonial works did. And yet he was not justified by this work; he was justified by faith. For Scripture says (Rom. 4:3): "Abraham believed God, and it was reckoned to him as righteousness."

"But after Christ was revealed," they say, "the ceremonial laws are fatal." Yes, the entire Law, including the Law of the Decalog, is also fatal without faith in Christ. Moreover, no Law should reign in the conscience except that of the Spirit of life, by which we are delivered in Christ from the Law of the letter and of death, from its works, and from sins. This does not mean that the Law is evil; it means that it cannot contribute anything to justification. It is something sublime and great to have a gracious God; and for this we need quite another Mediator than Moses or the Law, other than our own will, indeed, other even than that grace which they call "the love of God." Here we are not obliged to do anything at all. The only thing necessary is that we accept the treasure that is Christ, grasped by faith in our hearts, even though we feel that we are completely filled with sins. Thus these words, "by faith in Christ," are very emphatic, not empty and vain, as the sophists think when they leap over them so boldly.

*Because by works of the Law shall no one be justified.*

Thus far the words have been those that Paul spoke to Peter. In them he has summarized the chief doctrine of Christianity, which makes true Christians. Now he shifts the address to the Galatians, to whom he is writing, and he concludes: "Since the situation is that we are justified by faith in Christ, it follows that by works of the Law shall no one be justified."

"Not all flesh"[22] is a Hebraism that sins against grammar. Thus Gen. 4:15 says: "Lest any who came upon him should kill him." The Greeks and the Latins do not speak this way. "Not everyone" means "no one," and "not all flesh" means "no flesh." But in Latin "not all flesh" sounds as though it meant "some flesh." But the Holy Spirit does not observe this strict rule of grammar.

Now in Paul "flesh" does not, as the sophists suppose, mean crass sins;[23] for these he usually calls by their explicit names, like adultery, fornication, uncleanness, etc. (Gal. 5:19 ff.). But by "flesh" Paul means here what Christ means in John 3:6: "That which is born of the flesh is flesh." Therefore "flesh" means the entire nature of man, with reason and all his powers. This flesh, he says, is not justified by works, not even by those of the Law. He is not saying: "The flesh is not justified by works against the Law, such as debauchery, drunkenness, etc." But he is saying: "It is not justified by works done in accordance with the Law, works that are good." For Paul, therefore, "flesh" means the highest righteousness, wisdom, worship, religion, understanding, and will of which the world is capable. Therefore the monk is not justified by his order, nor the priest by the Mass and the canonical hours, nor the philosopher by wisdom, nor the theologian by theology, nor the Turk by the Koran, nor the Jew by Moses. In other words, no matter how wise and righteous men may be according to reason and the divine Law, yet with all their works, merits, Masses, righteousnesses, and acts of worship they are not justified.

The papists do not believe this. In their blindness and stubbornness, they defend their abominations against their own consciences. They persist in this blasphemy of theirs and still boast in these sacrilegious words: "Whoever does this or that merits the forgiveness of sins; whoever serves this or that holy order, to him we give a sure promise of eternal life." To take what Paul, the apostle of Christ, refuses to ascribe to the divine Law and its works, and to attribute this to the doctrines of demons (1 Tim. 4:1), to the statutes and rules of men, to the wicked traditions of the pope, and to the works of monks—this is an unspeakable and horrible blasphemy! For if, according to the testimony of the apostle, no one is justified by the works of the divine Law, much less will anyone be justified by the rule of Benedict, Francis, etc., in which there is not a syllable about faith in Christ but only the insistence that whoever observes these things has eternal life.

Therefore I have wondered a great deal that with these destructive heresies persisting for so many centuries the church could still endure amid such great darkness and error. There were some whom God called simply by the text of the Gospel, which nevertheless continued in the pulpit, and by Baptism. They walked in simplicity and humility of heart; they thought that the monks and those whom the bishops had ordained were the only ones who were religious and holy, while they themselves were profane and secular and therefore not to be compared with them. Since they found in themselves no good works or merits to pit against the wrath and judgment of God, they took refuge in the suffering and death of Christ; and in that simplicity they were saved.

The wrath of God is horrible and infinite, that for so many centuries He has been punishing the ingratitude and contempt of the Gospel and of Christ in the papists by giving them up to a reprobate mind (Rom. 1:24 ff.). Denying Christ completely and blaspheming Him in His saving work, they received, in place of the Gospel, the abomination of these rules and human traditions. These they treated with special reverence and preferred to the Word of God, until finally matrimony was forbidden them, and they were forced into an incestuous celibacy, in which they were outwardly polluted with all sorts of horrible vices—adultery, prostitution, impurity, sodomy, etc. This was the fruit of that impure celibacy. In His righteousness God gave them up to a reprobate mind inwardly, and outwardly

He permitted them to fall into such great crimes because they had blasphemed the only Son of God, in whom the Father wants to be glorified and whom He gave into death in order that all who believe in the Son might be saved by Him, and not by their orders. "Those who honor Me," He says (1 Sam. 2:30), "I will honor." Now God is honored in the Son (John 5:23). Therefore whoever believes that the Son is our Mediator and Savior, honors the Father; and God honors Him in turn, that is, adorns him with His gifts of the forgiveness of sins, righteousness, the Holy Spirit, and eternal life. But, on the other hand, "those who despise Me shall be lightly esteemed" (1 Sam. 2:30).

Therefore this is a universal principle: "By works of the Law shall no one be justified." Enlarge on this by running through all the stations of life as follows: "Therefore a monk shall not be justified by his order, a nun by her chastity, a citizen by his uprightness, a prince by his generosity, etc." The Law of God is greater than the entire world, since it includes all men; and the works of the Law are far more excellent than the works chosen by self-righteous people. And yet Paul says that neither the Law nor the works of the Law justify. Therefore faith alone justifies. Once this proposition is established, he proceeds to confirm it with further arguments. The first argument is "from a denial of the conclusion":[24]

> 17. *But if, in our endeavor to be justified in Christ, we ourselves were found to be sinners, is Christ then an agent of sin? Certainly not!*

These are not Latin phrases; they are Hebrew and theological. "If it is true," he says, "that we are justified in Christ, then it is impossible for us to be sinners or to be justified through the Law. On the other hand, if this is not true and we must be justified through the Law and its works, then it is impossible for us to be justified through Christ. One of these two has to be false: Either we are not justified in Christ, or we are not justified in the Law. But we are justified in Christ.

Therefore we are not justified in the Law." Thus he is arguing in this way: "If, in our endeavor, etc." That is: "If we try to be justified through faith in Christ, and, being justified in this way, are still found to be sinners who need the Law to justify us because we are sinners; if, I say, we need the observance of the Law for justification, so that those who are righteous in Christ are not really righteous but need the Law to justify them; or if he who is justified through Christ still has to be justified through the Law—then Christ is nothing but a law-giver and an agent of sin. Then he who is justified and holy in Christ is not justified or holy but is still in need of the righteousness and holiness of the Law.

"But we are surely justified and righteous in Christ, because the truth of the Gospel teaches that a man is not justified in the Law but is justified in Christ. But if those who are justified in Christ are still found to be sinners, that is, if they still belong to the Law and are under the Law, as the false apostles teach, then they are not yet justified. For the Law accuses them, shows that they are still sinners, and demands that they do the works of the Law to be justified. Therefore those who are justified in Christ are not justified; and so it necessarily follows that Christ is not a justifier, but an agent of sin."

Here he accuses the false apostles and all self-righteous people most gravely of perverting everything: They change Law into grace and grace into Law, Moses into Christ and Christ into Moses. For they teach that after Christ and all the righteousness of Christ the observance of the Law is necessary for one to be justified. By this intolerable perversity the Law becomes Christ; for they attribute to the Law what properly belongs to Christ. "If you do the works of the Law," they say, "you will be justified. But if you do not do them, you will not be justified, regardless of how much you believe in Christ." Now if it is true that Christ does not justify but is an agent of sin, as must necessarily follow from their teaching, then Christ is the Law; for since He teaches that we are sinners, we have nothing else from Him than what we have from the

Law. Thus Christ, the teacher of sin, sends us to the Law and
to Moses, the justifier!

Therefore it is inevitable that the papists, the Zwinglians,
the Anabaptists, and all those who either do not know about
the righteousness of Christ or who do not believe correctly
about it should change Christ into Moses and the Law and
change the Law into Christ. For this is what they teach: "Faith
in Christ does indeed justify, but at the same time observance
of the Commandments of God is necessary; for it is written
(Matt. 19:17): 'If you would enter life, keep the Commandments.'" Here immediately Christ is denied and faith is abolished, because what belongs to Christ alone is attributed to
the Commandments of God or to the Law. For Christ is, by
definition, the Justifier and the Redeemer from sins. If I attribute this to the Law, then the Law is my justifier, which
delivers me from my sins before I do its works. And so the
Law has now become Christ; and Christ completely loses
His name, His work, and His glory, and is nothing else than
an agent of the Law, who accuses, terrifies, directs, and sends
the sinner to someone else to be justified. This is really the
work of the Law.

But the work of Christ, properly speaking, is this: to em-
brace the one whom the Law has made a sinner and pronounced guilty, and to absolve him from his sins if he believes
the Gospel. "For Christ is the end of the Law, that everyone
who has faith may be justified" (Rom. 10:4); He is "the Lamb
of God, who takes away the sin of the world" (John 1:29).
But the papists and the fanatics turn this upside down; and
it is inevitable that they should, since they do not believe
correctly about the doctrine of justification and teach the very
opposite, namely, that Moses is Christ and Christ is Moses.
This is their main proposition. Then they ridicule us for in-
culcating and emphasizing faith with such diligence: "Ha, ha!
Faith, faith! Just wait until you get to heaven by faith! No,
you must strive for something more sublime. You must fulfill
the Law of God, according to the statement (Luke 10:28):

'Do this, and you will live.' You must suffer many things, shed your blood, forsake your house, wife, and children, and imitate the example of Christ. This faith of yours makes men smug, lazy, and sleepy." So they have become nothing but legalists and Mosaists, defecting from Christ to Moses and calling the people back from Baptism, faith, and the promises of Christ to the Law and works, changing grace into the Law and the Law into grace.

Who would ever believe that these things could be mixed up so easily? There is no one so stupid that he does not recognize how definite this distinction between Law and grace is. Both the facts and the words require this distinction, for everyone understands that these words "Law" and "grace" are different as to both denotation and connotation.[25] Therefore it is a monstrosity, when this distinction stands there so clearly, for the papists and the fanatics to fall into the satanic perversity of confusing the Law and grace and of changing Christ into Moses. This is why I often say that so far as the words are concerned, this doctrine of faith is very easy, and everyone can easily understand the distinction between the Law and grace; but so far as practice, life, and application are concerned, it is the most difficult thing there is.

The pope and his scholastic theologians say clearly that the Law and grace are distinct things, but in his practice he teaches the very opposite. "Faith in Christ," he says, "whether it is acquired by man's natural powers, actions, and qualities or whether it is infused by God, is still dead if love does not follow." What has happened to the distinction between the Law and grace? He distinguishes them in name, but in practice he calls grace love. Thus the sectarians demand works in addition to faith. Therefore anyone who does not believe correctly about the doctrine of justification must necessarily confuse Law and grace.

Let everyone who is godly, therefore, learn to distinguish carefully between Law and grace, both in feeling and in practice, not only in words, as the pope and the fanatics do. So far as the words are concerned, they admit that the two are distinct things; but in fact, as I have said, they confuse them, because they do not concede that faith justifies without works. If this is true, then Christ is of no use to me. For though I may have as true a faith as possible, yet, according to their opinion, I am not justified if this faith of mine is without love; and however much of this love I may have, it is never enough. Thus the Christ whom faith grasps is not the Justifier; grace is useless; and faith cannot be true without love—or, as the Anabaptists say, without the cross, suffering, and bloodshed.[26] But if love, works, and the cross are present, then faith is true, and it justifies.

With this doctrine the fanatics obscure the blessings of Christ today; they deprive Him of His honor as the Justifier and set Him up as an agent of sin. They have learned nothing from us except to recite the words; they do not accept the content. They want to give the impression that they, too, teach the Gospel and faith in Christ as purely as we do; but when it comes to the practice, they are teachers of the Law, just like the false apostles. Throughout all the churches the false apostles required, in addition to faith in Christ, that there be circumcision and the observance of the Law, without which they denied that faith could justify. "Unless you are circumcised according to the custom of Moses," they said, "you cannot be saved" (Acts 15:1). In the same way today the sectarians require, in addition to the righteousness of faith, the observance of the Commandments of God. They cite these passages: "Do this, and you will live" (Luke 10:28) and "If you would enter life, keep the Commandments" (Matt. 19:17).[27] Therefore there is no one among them, though he seem ever so wise, who understands the distinction between Law and grace; for they are convicted by their own practice and by the evidence of the facts.

But we do make a distinction here; and we say that we are not disputing now whether good works ought to be done. Nor are we inquiring whether the Law is good, holy, and righteous, or whether it ought to be observed; for that is another topic. But our argument and question concerns justification and whether the Law justifies. Our opponents do not listen to this. They do not answer this question, nor do they distinguish as we do. All they do is to scream that good works ought to be done and that the Law ought to be observed. All right, we know that. But because these are distinct topics, we will not permit them to be confused. In due time we shall discuss the teaching that the Law and good works ought to be done. But since we are now dealing with the subject of justification, we reject works, on which our opponents insist so tenaciously that they ascribe justification to them, which is to take Christ's glory away from Him and to assign it to works instead.

Therefore this is a powerful argument, which I have often used to console myself: "If in our endeavor, etc." It is as though Paul were saying: "If we who are justified in Christ are still regarded as not justified but as sinners who still need to be justified by the Law, then we cannot look for justification in Christ; then we look for it in the Law. But if justification happens through the Law, then it does not happen through grace. This is proved by sufficient division.[28] Now if justification does not happen through grace but happens through the Law, what did Christ accomplish with His suffering, His preaching, His victory over sin and death, and the sending of the Holy Spirit? Either we are justified through Christ, or we are made sinful and guilty through Him. But if the Law justifies, then it follows inevitably that we become sinners through Christ; and so Christ is an agent of sin. So let us establish the proposition: Everyone who believes in the Lord Jesus Christ is a sinner and is worthy of eternal death; and if he does not have recourse to the Law and do its works, he will not be saved."

Holy Scripture, especially the New Testament, always inculcates faith in Christ and magnificently proclaims Him. It says that "whoever believes in Him is saved, does not perish, is not judged, is not put to shame, and has eternal life" (John

3:16). But they say, on the contrary: "Whoever believes in Him is damned, etc., because he has faith without works, which damns." This is how they pervert everything, making Christ the condemner and Moses the savior. Is it not an unspeakable blasphemy to teach this way: "By performing the Law and works you will become worthy of eternal life, but by believing in Christ you will become worthy of eternal death. When the Law is kept, it saves; and faith in Christ damns"?

Of course, our opponents do not use these very words; but this is actually what they teach. For they say that "infused faith," which they properly call faith in Christ, does not free from sin, but that only "faith formed by love" does so. From this it follows that faith in Christ by itself, without the Law and works, does not save. Surely this is to declare that Christ leaves us in our sins and in the wrath of God and makes us worthy of eternal death. On the other hand, if you perform the Law and works, then faith justifies, because it has works, without which faith is useless. Therefore works justify, not faith. That because of which something is what it is, is itself more so. For if faith justifies because of works, then works justify more than faith. How deep the abominable blasphemy of this doctrine is!

Therefore Paul is arguing from the impossible and from a sufficient division.[29] If we who are justified in Christ are still sinners who must be justified otherwise than through Christ, namely, through the Law, then Christ cannot justify us but only accuses and condemns us. Then Christ died in vain, and these and similar passages are false: "Behold, the Lamb of God, etc." (John 1:29); "He who believes in the Son has eternal life" (John 3:36). Then all Scripture is false when it testifies that Christ is the Justifier and the Savior. For if we are still sinners after being justified in Christ, then it necessarily follows that those who do the Law without Christ are justified. If this is true, then we are Turks or Jews or Tartars, who keep the Word and name of Christ for the sake of external appearances, but who, in practice and in fact, completely deny Christ and His Word. But Paul wants faith to be ἀνυπόκριτον (1 Tim. 1:5). Therefore it is wrong and wicked to assert that infused faith does not justify unless it is adorned with works of love. But if our opponents feel obliged to defend this doctrine, then why do they not reject faith in Christ completely, especially since they make it nothing but an empty quality in the soul, which is worthless without love? Why do they not call a spade a spade?[30] In other words, why do they not say in clear words that works, not faith, justify? Why do they not publicly deny the entire Gospel and Paul—as they do in fact—who attribute righteousness to faith alone and not to works? For if faith justifies only with love, then Paul's argument is completely false; for he says clearly that a man is not justified by works of the Law, but alone by faith in Jesus Christ.

*Is Christ then an agent of sin?*

"Minister of sin"[31] is once more a Hebrew phrase, which Paul uses also in 2 Cor. 3:7 ff., where he discusses these two ministries so magnificently and clearly, namely, the ministry of the letter and of the spirit, of the Law and of grace, of death and of life. And he says that Moses, the minister of the Law, has the ministry of the Law, which he calls a ministry of sin, wrath, death, and damnation. For Paul usually employs terms of reproach for the Law of God. He is the only one of the apostles to use this phrase; the others do not speak this way. It is important for those who are students of Sacred Scripture to understand this phrase of Paul.

Now a "minister of sin" is nothing else but a lawgiver, a teacher of the Law, or a taskmaster, who teaches good works and love; he teaches that one should bear the cross and suffering, and that one should imitate Christ and the saints. Anyone who teaches and demands this is a minister of the Law as well as of sin, wrath, and death, because all he does by his doctrine is to terrify and trouble consciences and to shut them up under sin. For it is impossible for human nature to fulfill the Law. In fact, in those who are justified and who have the Holy Spirit the law in their members is at war with the law of their mind (Rom. 7:23). Then what would it not do in the wicked, who do not have the Holy Spirit? Therefore anyone who teaches that righteousness comes through the Law does not understand what he is saying or what he is propounding; much less does he observe the Law. Instead, he is fooling himself and others, imposing an unbearable burden upon them, prescribing and demanding something impossible, and ultimately bringing himself and his followers to the point of despair.

Therefore the proper use and aim of the Law is to make guilty those who are smug and at peace, so that they may see that they are in danger of sin, wrath, and death, so that they may be terrified and despairing, blanching and quaking at the rustling of a leaf (Lev. 26:36).[32] To the extent that they are such, they are under the Law. For the Law requires perfect obedience toward God, and it damns those who do not yield such obedience. Now it is certain that no one yields this obedience or even can; nevertheless, this is what God wants. Therefore the Law does not justify; it condemns. For it says (Gal. 3:10): "Cursed be everyone who does not abide, etc." Therefore one who teaches the Law is a "minister of sin."

In 2 Cor. 3:7, therefore, Paul correctly calls the ministry of the Law a "ministry of sin." For the Law does nothing but accuse consciences and manifest sin, which is dead without the Law. The knowledge of sin—I am not speaking about the speculative knowledge that hypocrites have; but I am speaking about true knowledge, in which the wrath of God against sin is perceived and a true taste of death is sensed—this knowledge terrifies hearts, drives them to despair, and kills them (Rom. 7:11). Scripture calls these teachers of the Law and works taskmasters and tyrants. The taskmasters in Egypt oppressed the Children of Israel with physical slavery. Thus with their doctrine of the Law and works these men drive souls into a miserable spiritual slavery, and eventually they push them into despair and destroy them. Nor is it possible for them to attain peace of conscience amid their genuine terrors and in the agony of death, although they have observed their monastic rule, loved others, performed many good works, and suffered evils; for the Law always terrifies and accuses, saying: "But you have not done enough!" Therefore these terrors still remain and become worse and worse. If these teachers of the Law are not raised up by faith and the righteousness of Christ, they are forced to despair.

There is an outstanding example of this in *The Lives of the Fathers*.[33] Shortly before he died, a certain hermit stood sad and motionless for three days, with his eyes fixed on heaven. When he was asked why he was doing this, he replied that he was afraid of death. Although his pupils tried to comfort him by saying that he had no reason to be afraid of death, since he had lived a very holy life, he responded: "I have indeed lived a holy life and observed the Commandments of God, but the judgments of God are quite different from those of men!" When this man saw that death was present, he was not able to be of a tranquil mind, even though he had lived blamelessly and had observed the Law of God; for it came to his mind that God judges much differently from men. Thus he lost confidence in all his good works and merits; and unless he was raised up by the promise of Christ, he despaired. So all the Law can do is to render us naked and guilty. Then there is no aid or counsel, but everything is lost. Here the lives and martyrdoms of all the saints cannot give us any help.

This was also beautifully foreshadowed in the story of the giving of the Law (Ex. 19–20). Moses led the people out of the camp to meet with the Lord and to hear Him speak from the darkness of the cloud. A little earlier the people had promised to do everything that the Lord commanded. Now they were afraid and trembled, and they ran back. Standing afar off, they said to Moses (Ex. 20:19): "Who can stand seeing the fire and hearing the thunder and the blare of the trumpet? You speak to us, and we will hear; but let not God speak to us, lest we die." Thus the proper task of the Law is to lead us forth from our tabernacles, that is, from our peace and self-confidence, to set us into the sight of God, and to reveal the wrath of God to us. Then the conscience senses that it has not satisfied the Law; it cannot satisfy the Law or bear the wrath of God, which the Law reveals when it sets us into the sight of God this way, that is, when it terrifies us, accuses us, and shows us our sins. Here it is impossible for us to stand. Thoroughly frightened, we run away and exclaim with Israel: "We are going to die, we are going to die! Let not the Lord speak, but you speak to us."

Therefore anyone who teaches that faith in Christ does not justify unless the Law is observed makes Christ a minister of sin, that is, a teacher of the Law, who teaches the same thing that Moses did. Then Christ is not the Savior and Dispenser of grace; but He is a cruel tyrant, who, like Moses, demands the impossible, which no man can produce. Thus Erasmus and the papists suppose that Christ is only a new lawgiver; and the fanatics accept nothing of the Gospel, except that they imagine it to be a book containing new laws about works, as the Turks imagine about their Koran.[34] But there are plenty of laws in Moses. The Gospel, however, is a proclamation about Christ: that He forgives sins, grants grace, justifies, and saves sinners. Although there are commandments in the Gospel, they are not the Gospel; they are expositions of the Law and appendices to the Gospel.

Thus if the Law is a ministry of sin, it follows that it is also a ministry of wrath and death. For just as the Law reveals sin, so it strikes the wrath of God into a man and threatens him with death. Immediately his conscience draws the inference: "You have not observed the Commandments; therefore God is offended and is angry with you." This logic is irrefutable: "I have sinned; therefore I shall die." Thus the ministry of sin is necessarily the ministry of the wrath of God and death. For where there is sin, there the conscience soon declares: "You have sinned; therefore God is angry with you. If

He is angry, He will kill you and damn you eternally." And this is why many who cannot endure the wrath and judgment of God commit suicide by hanging or drowning.

20. *I have been crucified with Christ.*

Paul adds this because he wants to declare that the Law is the devourer of the Law. "Not only am I dead to the Law through the Law so that I might live to God," he says, "but I am also crucified with Christ. But Christ is the Lord of the Law, because He has been crucified and has died to the Law. Therefore I, too, am lord of the Law. For I, too, have been crucified and have died to the Law, since I have been crucified and have died with Christ." How? Through grace and faith. When by this faith I am crucified and die to the Law, then the Law loses all its jurisdiction over me, as it lost it over Christ. Thus, just as Christ Himself was crucified to the Law, sin, death, and the devil, so that they have no further jurisdiction over Him, so through faith I, having been crucified with Christ in spirit, am crucified and die to the Law, sin, etc., so that they have no further jurisdiction over me but are now crucified and dead to me.

But here Paul is not speaking about being crucified with Christ by imitation or example—for imitating the example of Christ is also being crucified with Him—which is a crucifixion that pertains to the flesh. 1 Peter 2:21 deals with this: "Christ suffered for you, leaving you an example, that you should follow in His steps." But he is speaking here about that sublime crucifixion by which sin, the devil, and death are crucified in Christ, not in me. Here Christ does everything alone. But I, as a believer, am crucified with Christ through faith, so that all these things are dead and crucified to me as well.

*Nevertheless, I live.*

Paul is speaking clearly and precisely. He says: "I am not speaking about my death and crucifixion as though I were not alive now. I am alive indeed, for I am made alive by the very death and crucifixion by which I die. That is, since I am liberated from the Law, sin, and death by grace and by faith, I am truly alive. Therefore the crucifixion and death by which I am crucified and die to the Law, sin, death, and all evils is resurrection and life to me. For Christ crucifies the devil, kills death, damns sin, and binds the Law. As one who believes this, I am liberated from the Law, etc. Therefore the Law is deaf, bound, dead, and crucified to me; and I, in turn, am deaf, bound, dead, and crucified to it. Thus I live by this very death and crucifixion, that is, by this grace or liberty." Here, as I have warned before, Paul's phraseology must be observed. He says that we die and are crucified to the Law, even though it is rather the Law itself that dies and is crucified to us. But he deliberately uses this phraseology and says that we are crucified and dead to the Law; he does so to make his language more pleasant. For although the Law still remains, lives, and rules in the whole world and accuses and condemns all men, it is crucified and dies only to believers in Christ. Therefore only they have the glory of being crucified and dead to the Law, sin, etc.

*Yet not I.*

That is, "not in my own person or substance." Here Paul clearly shows how he is alive; and he states what Christian righteousness is, namely, that righteousness by which Christ lives in us, not the righteousness that is in our own person. Therefore when it is necessary to discuss Christian righteousness, the person must be completely rejected. For if I pay attention to the person or speak of the person, then, whether intentionally or unintentionally on my part, the person becomes a doer of works who is subject to the Law. But here Christ and my conscience must become one body, so that nothing remains in my sight but Christ, crucified and risen. But if Christ is put aside and I look only at myself, then I am done for. For then this thought immediately comes to my mind: "Christ is in heaven, and you are on earth. How are you now going to reach Him?" "I will live a holy life and do what the Law requires; and in this way I shall enter life." By

paying attention to myself and considering what my condition
is or should be, and what I am supposed to be doing, I lose
sight of Christ, who alone is my Righteousness and Life. Once
He is lost, there is no aid or counsel; but certain despair and
perdition must follow.

This is an extremely common evil; for such is human misery
that in temptation or death we immediately put Christ aside
and pay attention to our own life and our own deeds. Unless
we are raised up here by faith, we must perish. In such conflicts
of conscience, therefore, we must form the habit of leaving
ourselves behind as well as the Law and all our works, which
force us to pay attention to ourselves. We must turn our eyes
completely to that bronze serpent, Christ nailed to the cross
(John 3:14). With our gaze fastened firmly to Him we must
declare with assurance that He is our Righteousness and Life
and care nothing about the threats and terrors of the Law,
sin, death, wrath, and the judgment of God. For the Christ
on whom our gaze is fixed, in whom we exist, and who also
lives in us, is the Victor and the Lord over the Law, sin, death,
and every evil. In Him a sure comfort has been set forth for
us, and victory has been granted.

*Nevertheless, I live; yet not I, but Christ lives in me.*

When he says: "Nevertheless, I live," this sounds rather
personal, as though Paul were speaking of his own person.
Therefore he quickly corrects it and says: "Yet not I." That
is, "I do not live in my own person now, but Christ lives in
me." The person does indeed live, but not in itself or for its
own person. But who is this "I" of whom he says: "Yet not
I"? It is the one that has the Law and is obliged to do works,
the one that is a person separate from Christ. This "I" Paul
rejects; for "I," as a person distinct from Christ, belongs to
death and hell. This is why he says: "Not I, but Christ lives
in me." Christ is my "form,"[35] which adorns my faith as color
or light adorns a wall. (This fact has to be expounded in this
crude way, for there is no spiritual way for us to grasp the idea
that Christ clings and dwells in us as closely and intimately

as light or whiteness clings to a wall.) "Christ," he says, "is
fixed and cemented to me and abides in me. The life that I
now live, He lives in me. Indeed, Christ Himself is the life that
I now live. In this way, therefore, Christ and I are one."

Living in me as He does, Christ abolishes the Law, damns
sin, and kills death; for at His presence all these cannot help
disappearing. Christ is eternal Peace, Comfort, Righteousness,
and Life, to which the terror of the Law, sadness of mind, sin,
hell, and death have to yield. Abiding and living in me, Christ
removes and absorbs all the evils that torment and afflict me.
This attachment to Him causes me to be liberated from the
terror of the Law and of sin, pulled out of my own skin, and
transferred into Christ and into His kingdom, which is a
kingdom of grace, righteousness, peace, joy, life, salvation,
and eternal glory. Since I am in Him, no evil can harm me.

Meanwhile my old man (Eph. 4:22) remains outside and
is subject to the Law. But so far as justification is concerned,
Christ and I must be so closely attached that He lives in me
and I in Him. What a marvelous way of speaking! Because
He lives in me, whatever grace, righteousness, life, peace, and
salvation there is in me is all Christ's; nevertheless, it is mine
as well, by the cementing and attachment that are through
faith, by which we become as one body in the Spirit. Since
Christ lives in me, grace, righteousness, life, and eternal salvation must be present with Him; and the Law, sin, and death
must be absent. Indeed, the Law must be crucified, devoured,
and abolished by the Law—and sin by sin, death by death,
the devil by the devil. In this way Paul seeks to withdraw us
completely from ourselves, from the Law, and from works,
and to transplant us into Christ and faith in Christ, so that
in the area of justification we look only at grace, and separate
it far from the Law and from works, which belong far away.

Paul has a peculiar phraseology—not human, but divine
and heavenly. The evangelists and the other apostles do not
use it, except for John, who speaks this way from time to time.
If Paul had not used this way of speaking first and prescribed

it for us in explicit terms, no one even among the saints would have dared[36] use it. It is unprecedented and insolent to say: "I live, I do not live; I am dead, I am not dead; I am a sinner, I am not a sinner; I have the Law, I do not have the Law." But this phraseology is true in Christ and through Christ. When it comes to justification, therefore, if you divide Christ's Person from your own, you are in the Law; you remain in it and live in yourself, which means that you are dead in the sight of God and damned by the Law. For you have a faith that is, as the sophists imagine, "formed by love." I am speaking this way for the sake of illustration. For there is no one who has such a faith; therefore what the sophists have taught about "faith formed by love" is merely a trick of Satan. But let us concede that a man could be found who had such a faith. Even if he had it, he would actually be dead, because he would have only a historical faith about Christ, something that even the devil and all the wicked have (James 2:19).

But faith must be taught correctly, namely, that by it you are so cemented to Christ that He and you are as one person, which cannot be separated but remains attached to Him forever and declares: "I am as Christ." And Christ, in turn, says: "I am as that sinner who is attached to Me, and I to him. For by faith we are joined together into one flesh and one bone." Thus Eph. 5:30 says: "We are members of the body of Christ, of His flesh and of His bones," in such a way that this faith couples Christ and me more intimately than a husband is coupled to his wife. Therefore this faith is no idle quality; but it is a thing of such magnitude that it obscures and completely removes those foolish dreams of the sophists' doctrine—the fiction of a "formed faith" and of love, of merits, our worthiness, our quality, etc. I would like to treat this at greater length if I could.

Thus far we have shown that Paul's first argument is this: Either Christ must be an agent of sin, or the Law does not justify. When this argument was concluded, he proposed himself as an example to develop a personification:[37] He said that he was dead to the old Law, on the basis of some sort of new Law. Now he attaches two replies to objections, or anticipations of his opponents' objections.[38] The first deals with slanders by proud men and with offense to weak men. When the free forgiveness of sins is preached, those who are malicious soon slander this preaching, as in Rom. 3:8: "Why not do evil that good may come?" For as soon as such men hear that we are not justified by the Law, they immediately infer slanderously: "Then let us forget about the Law." Or they say: "If grace is superabundant where sin was abundant, then let us be abundant in sin, so that we may be justified and grace may be superabundant." These are the spiteful and arrogant men who willfully distort Scripture and the sayings of the Holy Spirit, as they distorted Paul during the lifetime of the apostles, "to their own destruction," as 2 Peter 3:16 says.

On the other hand, the weak, who are not malicious or slanderous but good, are offended when they hear that the Law and good works do not have to be done for justification. One must go to their aid and explain to them how it is that works do not justify, how works should be done, and how they should not be done. They should be done as fruits of righteousness, not in order to bring righteousness into being. Having been made righteous, we must do them; but it is not the other way around: that when we are unrighteous, we become righteous by doing them. The tree produces fruit; the fruit does not produce the tree.

Paul had said above: "I have died, etc." Here a malicious person could easily cavil and say: "What are you saying, Paul? Are you dead? Then how is it that you are speaking and writing?" A weak person might also be easily offended and say: "Who are you anyway? Do I not see you alive and doing things?" He replies: "I do indeed live; and yet not I live, but Christ lives in me. There is a double life: my own, which is natural or animate; and an alien life, that of Christ in me.[39] So far as my animate life is concerned, I am dead and am now living an alien life. I am not living as Paul now, for Paul

is dead." Who, then, is living? "The Christian." Paul, living in
himself, is utterly dead through the Law but living in Christ,
or rather with Christ living in him, he lives an alien life. Christ
is speaking, acting, and performing all actions in him; these
belong not to the Paul-life, but to the Christ-life. "You malicious person, do not slander me for saying that I am dead.
And you weak person, do not be offended, but make the
proper distinction. There is a double life, my life and an alien
life. By my own life I am not living; for if I were, the Law
would have dominion over me and would hold me captive.
To keep it from holding me, I am dead to it by another Law.
And this death acquires an alien life for me, namely, the life
of Christ, which is not inborn in me but is granted to me in
faith through Christ."

The second reply to objections. This objection, too, could
have been raised against Paul: "What are you saying? You do
not live by your own life or in the flesh; you live in Christ?
To be sure, I see your flesh; but I do not see Christ. Are you
trying to deceive us by some trick into not seeing that you are
present in the flesh, living your familiar life, having five senses,
and doing everything in this physical life that any other man
does?" He replies:

*And the life I now live in the flesh I live by faith in the Son
of God.*

That is to say: "I do indeed live in the flesh; but this life
that is being led within me, whatever it is, I do not regard as
a life. For actually it is not a true life but only a mask of life,
under which there lives another One, namely, Christ, who is
truly my Life. This life you do not see; you only hear it as 'you
hear the sound of the wind, but you do not know whence it
comes or whither it goes' (John 3:8). Thus you see me talking,
eating, working, sleeping, etc.; and yet you do not see my
life. For the time of life that I am living I do indeed live in the
flesh, but not on the basis of the flesh and according to the
flesh, but in faith, on the basis of faith, and according to faith."
He does not deny that he lives in the flesh, for he is doing all

the works of an animate man. Besides, he is also using physical things—food, clothing, etc.—which is surely living in the flesh. But he says that this is not his life, and that he does not live according to these things. He does indeed use physical things; but he does not live by them, as the world lives on the basis of the flesh and according to the flesh, because it neither knows nor hopes for any life besides this physical life.

"Therefore," says Paul, "whatever this life is that I now live in the flesh, I live by faith in the Son of God." That is, the Word I speak physically is not the word of the flesh; it is the Word of the Holy Spirit and of Christ. The vision that enters or leaves my eyes does not come from the flesh; that is, my flesh does not direct it, but the Holy Spirit does. Thus hearing does not come from the flesh, even though it is in the flesh; but it is in and from the Holy Spirit. A Christian speaks nothing but chaste, sober, holy, and divine things—things that pertain to Christ, the glory of God, and the salvation of his neighbor. These things do not come from the flesh, nor are they done according to the flesh; nevertheless, they are in the flesh. I cannot teach, preach, write, pray, or give thanks except by these physical instruments, which are required for the performance of these activities. Nevertheless, these activities do not come from the flesh and do not originate there; they are given and revealed divinely from heaven. Thus also I look at a woman with my eyes, yet with a chaste vision and not in desire for her. Such vision does not come from the flesh, even though it is in the flesh; the eyes are the physical instrument of the vision, but the chastity of the vision comes from heaven.

Thus a Christian uses the world and all its creatures in such a way that there is no difference between him and an ungodly man. Their food and clothing are the same; their hearing, vision, and speaking are the same; their gestures, appearance, and shape are the same. Thus Paul also says about Christ: "being found in human form" (Phil. 2:8). Nevertheless, there is the greatest possible difference. I do indeed live in the flesh, but I do not live on the basis of my own self. The life I now live in the flesh I live by faith in the Son of God. What you now hear me speak proceeds from another source than what you heard me speak before. Before his conversion Paul spoke with the same voice and tongue. But his voice and his tongue were blasphemous then; therefore he could not speak anything but blasphemies and abominations against God. After his conversion his flesh, tongue, and voice were the same as they had been before; nothing at all was changed. But now the voice and tongue did not speak blasphemies; now it spoke spiritual words of thanksgiving and praise for God, which came from faith and from the Holy Spirit. Thus I do live in the flesh, yet not on the basis of the flesh or according to the flesh but by faith in the Son of God.

From all this it is evident whence this alien and spiritual life comes. The unspiritual man does not perceive this, because he does not know what sort of life this is. He "hears the sound of the wind, but he does not know whence it comes or whither it goes" (John 3:8). He hears the voice of the spiritual man; he recognizes his face, his habits, and his gestures. But whence these words come, which are not sacrilegious or blasphemous now but holy and divine, and whence these motives and actions come—this he does not see. For this life is in the heart through faith. There the flesh is extinguished; and there Christ rules with His Holy Spirit, who now sees, hears, speaks, works, suffers, and does simply everything in him, even though the flesh is still reluctant. In short, this life is not the life of the flesh, although it is a life in the flesh; but it is the life of Christ, the Son of God, whom the Christian possesses by faith.

*Who loved me and gave Himself for me.*

Here you have the true meaning of justification described, together with an example of the certainty of faith. "I live by faith in the Son of God, who loved me and gave Himself for me"—anyone who could say these words with Paul in a certain and constant faith would be truly blessed. With these very words Paul completely abrogates and removes the righteousness of the Law and of works, as we shall point out later.

Therefore these words must be diligently pondered: "The Son of God loved me and gave Himself for me." It was not I who loved the Son of God and gave myself for Him, as the sophists pretend that they love the Son of God and give themselves for Him. For they teach that purely by his natural endowments[40] a man is able to perform the "merit of congruity" and to love God and Christ above all things. They anticipate the love of God and of Christ by doing what lies within them; they become monks and observe poverty, chastity, and obedience. Thus they dream that they give themselves for Christ. They turn the words of Paul upside down and read them this way: "We have loved Christ and have given ourselves for Him." But while these wicked men, inflated with the mind of their own flesh, dream and imagine that they are doing what lies within them, loving God and giving themselves for Christ, they actually abolish the Gospel, ridicule, deny, blaspheme, spit upon, and tread Christ underfoot. In words they confess that He is the Justifier and the Savior; but in fact they deprive Him of the power either to justify or to save, and they attribute this to their self-chosen acts of worship. This is not living by faith in the Son of God; it is living by one's own righteousness and works.

Therefore the true way of being justified is not that you begin "to do what lies within you"; that is the phraseology they use. "If a man," they say, "does what lies within him, God infallibly gives him grace."[41] That proposition is extremely important. In fact, it is an article of faith among the sophists. They do, however, tone down the statement "to do what lies within one" by saying that this is not to be taken as an indivisible or mathematical point but as a physical one. That is, it is enough if a man does what can be approved by the judgment of a good man. This need not be judged by an indivisible point, since it is impossible for any such to exist; but it is enough for the point to be approximate. In other words, it is enough that someone acts, fasts, etc., in a way that would be said to be good according to the judgment of a good man. Then grace would certainly follow, not by the merit of congruity itself but by the infallibility of God, who is so good and just that He cannot help granting grace in exchange for something good. And this was the origin of the little verse:

> God does not require of any man
> That he do more than he really can.[42]

This is actually a good statement, but in its proper place, that is, in political, domestic, and natural affairs. For example, if I, who exist in the realm of reason, rule a family, build a house, or carry on a governmental office, and I do as much as I can or what lies within me, I am excused. For this realm has boundaries, and to this realm these statements like "to do what lies within one" or "to do as much as I can" properly apply. But the sophists drag these statements into the spiritual realm, where a man cannot do anything but sin, because he is "sold under sin" (Rom. 7:14). But in external matters, that is, in political and domestic affairs, man is not a slave but a lord of these physical matters. Therefore it was wicked of the sophists to drag these political and domestic statements into the church. For the realm of human reason must be separated as far as possible from the spiritual realm.

They have also handed down the statement that human nature has been corrupted, but that its natural endowments are sound; these latter they attributed also to the demons. But since the natural endowments are sound, the intellect is pure, and the will is good and sound; and thus, by logical consistency, everything is perfect. It is necessary to know these things if the purity of the doctrine of faith is to be preserved. When the sophists say that the natural endowments are sound, I concede this. But if they draw the inference: "Therefore a man is able to fulfill the Law, to love God, etc.," then I deny the conclusion. I distinguish the natural endowments from the spiritual; and I say that the spiritual endowments are not sound but corrupt, in fact, totally extinguished through sin in man and in the devil. Thus there is nothing there but a depraved intellect and a will that is hostile and opposed to God's will—a will that thinks nothing except what is against God. The natural endowments are indeed sound, but which natural endowments? Those by which a man who is drowned in wickedness and is a slave of the devil has a will, reason, free choice, and power to build a house, to carry on a governmental office, to steer a ship, and to do other tasks that have been made subject to man according to Gen. 1:28; these have not been taken away from man. Procreation, government, and the home have not been abolished by such statements; they have been confirmed. But the sophists twisted them into the spiritual realm. Perhaps they received them from the fathers. But because they understood them poorly, they distorted them to apply to spiritual affairs; thus they confused civil and ecclesiastical matters. It is up to us to clean this up and to remove these scandals from the church. We concede that these statements are true, but in their proper place, that is, in the physical realm. But if you drag them into the spiritual realm before the sight of God, we completely deny them. For there we are completely drowned in sins. Whatever is in our will is evil; whatever is in our intellect is error. In divine matters, therefore, man has nothing but darkness, error, malice, and perversity of will and of intellect. Then how could he do good works, love God, etc.?

Therefore Paul says here that not we but Christ took the initiative. "He loved me," he says, "and gave Himself for me." It is as though he were saying: "He did not find a good will or a correct intellect in me, but He Himself took pity on me. He saw that I was ungodly, erring, turned away from God, drawing back and fighting against God; and that I had been captured, directed, and steered by the devil. By a mercy that preceded my reason, will, and intellect He loved me, and loved me so much that He gave Himself for me, that I might be delivered from the Law, sin, the devil, and death."

These words, "the Son of God," "He loved me," and "He gave Himself for me," are sheer thunder and heavenly fire against the righteousness of the Law and the doctrine of works. There was such great evil, such great error, and such darkness and ignorance in my will and intellect that I could be liberated only by such an inestimable price. Then why do we boast about the rule of reason, about our sound natural endowments, about reason's preference for the best things, and about doing what lies within one? Why do I offer to a wrathful God, who is, as Moses says, "a devouring fire" (Deut. 4:24), some straw, in fact, my horrible sins, and want to demand of Him that in exchange for them He grant me grace and eternal life? For I hear in this passage that there is so much evil in my nature that the world and all creation would not suffice to placate God, but that the Son of God Himself had to be given up for it.

But consider this price carefully, and look at this captive, the Son of God. You will see then that He is greater[43] and more excellent than all creation. What will you do when you hear Paul say that such an inestimable price was given for your sins? Will you bring your cowl or tonsure or chastity or obedience or poverty? What are all these? Indeed, what is the Law of Moses and the works of the Law? What are all the works of all men and the sufferings of the martyrs? What is all the obedience of the holy angels compared with the Son of God "given," and given in the most shameful way, into death, even death on a cross (Phil. 2:8), so that all His most precious blood was shed—and for your sins? If you looked at this price, you would take all your cowls, tonsures, vows, works, merits of congruity, and merits of condignity, and you would curse, defile, spit upon, and damn them, and consign them to hell! Therefore it is an intolerable and horrible blasphemy to think up some work by which you presume to placate God, when you see that He cannot be placated except by this immense, infinite price, the death and the blood of the Son of God, one drop of which is more precious than all creation.[44]

*For me.*

Who is this "me"? It is I,[45] an accursed and damned sinner, who was so beloved by the Son of God that He gave Himself for me. Therefore if I could have loved the Son of God and come to Him by works or by merits of congruity and condignity, what need would there have been for Him to give Himself for me? From this it is evident how coldly the papists treated the Holy Scriptures and the teaching of faith, in fact, how they completely neglected them. For if they had only looked at these words, that the Son of God had to be given for me, it would have been impossible for any order or sect to arise, because faith would have replied immediately: "Why are you choosing this way of life, this order, this work? Is it so that God may be placated or that you may be justified? You scoundrel, do you not hear that the Son of God was given and that He shed His blood for you?" Thus faith in Christ would have been able very easily to resist all sects.

Therefore I say that there is no force that can resist the sects, and no remedy against them except this one doctrine of Christian righteousness. If this doctrine is lost, it is impossible for us to be able to resist any errors or sects. We can see this today in the fanatics, Anabaptists, and Sacramentarians. Now that they have fallen away from this doctrine, they will never stop falling, erring, and seducing others ad infinitum. Undoubtedly they will arouse innumerable sects and think up new works. Although in outward appearance all these things may be very good and saintly, what are they in comparison with the death and the blood of the Son of God, who gave Himself for me? Who is this Son of God? What are heaven and earth in comparison with Him? Rather than that the truth of the Gospel should be obscured and the glory of Christ perish, let all the fanatics and papists go to hell, with all their righteousnesses, works, and merits—even if the whole world should be on their side! Then why is it that they brag about works and merits? If I, an accursed and damned sinner, could be redeemed by some other price, what need was there that the Son of God should be given for me? But because there was no price in heaven or on earth except Christ, the Son of God, therefore it was extremely necessary that He be given for me. He also did this because of His great love; for Paul says: "who loved me."

Now these words, "who loved me," are filled with faith. Anyone who can speak this brief pronoun "me" in faith and apply it to himself as Paul did, will, like Paul, be the best of debaters against the Law. For He did not give a sheep or an ox or gold or silver for me. But He who was completely God gave everything He was, gave Himself for me—for me, I say, a miserable and accursed sinner. I am revived by this "giving" of the Son of God into death, and I apply it to myself. This applying is the true power of faith. One who performs works does not say: "Christ loved me, etc."

Paul opposes these words, which are the purest proclamation of grace and of Christian righteousness, to the righteousness of the Law. It is as though he were saying: "All right, let the Law be a divine teaching and let it have its glory. It still did not love me or give itself for me, but it accuses and frightens me. Now I have Another, who has freed me from the terrors of the Law, from sin, and from death, and who has transferred me into freedom, the righteousness of God, and eternal life. He is called the Son of God, who loved me and gave Himself for me."

As I have said, faith grasps and embraces Christ, the Son of God, who was given for us, as Paul teaches here. When He has been grasped by faith, we have righteousness and life. For Christ is the Son of God, who gave Himself out of sheer love to redeem me. In these words Paul gives a beautiful description of the priesthood and the work of Christ, which is to placate God, to intercede and pray for sinners, to offer Himself as a sacrifice for their sins, and to redeem them. Therefore you should learn to define Christ properly, not as the sophists and fanatics do; they make of Him a new lawgiver who, after abrogating the old Law, established a new Law. For them Christ is a taskmaster and a tyrant. But you should define Him as Paul does here, as the Son of God, who, not because of merit or any righteousness of ours, but because of His sheer mercy and love, gave and offered Himself to God as a sacrifice for us miserable sinners, to sanctify us forever.

Therefore Christ is not Moses, not a taskmaster or a lawgiver; He is the Dispenser of grace, the Savior, and the Pitier. In other words, He is nothing but sheer, infinite mercy, which gives and is given. Then you will depict Christ correctly. If you let Him be depicted to you any other way, you will soon be overthrown in the hour of temptation. The highest art among Christians is to be able to define Christ this way; it is also the most difficult of arts. For it is very hard for me, even in the great light of the Gospel and after my extensive experience and practice in this study, to define Christ as Paul does here. That is how much this teaching and noxious idea of Christ as the lawgiver has penetrated into my bones like oil. On this score you younger men are much more fortunate than we older ones.[46] You have not been imbued with these noxious ideas with which I was imbued from boyhood, so that even at the mention of the name of Christ I would be terrified and grow pale, because I was persuaded that He was a judge. Therefore I have to make a double effort: first, to unlearn, condemn, and resist this ingrown opinion of Christ as a lawgiver and a judge, which constantly returns and drags me back; secondly, to acquire a new idea, namely, trust in Christ as the Justifier and the Savior. If you are willing, you can have much less difficulty learning to know Christ purely. Therefore if any sadness or tribulation afflicts one's heart, this should not be ascribed to Christ, even though it may come under the name of Christ, but to the devil, who makes a practice of coming under the name of Christ and of disguising himself as an angel of light (2 Cor. 11:14).

Therefore let us learn to distinguish carefully between Christ and a lawgiver, not only in word but also in fact and in practice. Then, when the devil comes, disguised as Christ and harassing us under His name, we will know that he is not Christ, but that he is really the devil. For Christ is the joy and sweetness of a trembling and troubled heart. We have this on the authority of Paul, who adorns Him with the sweetest of titles here, calling Him the One "who loved *me*[47] and gave Himself for me." Therefore Christ is the Lover of those who are in anguish, sin, and death, and the kind of Lover who gives Himself for us and becomes our High Priest, that is, the One who interposes Himself as the Mediator between God and us miserable sinners. I ask you what could be said that would be more joyful and happy than this? If all this is true—and it must be true, or otherwise the whole Gospel is false—then surely we are not justified by the righteousness of the Law, much less by our own righteousness.

Therefore read these words "*me*" and "*for me*" with great emphasis, and accustom yourself to accepting this "*me*" with a sure faith and applying it to yourself. Do not doubt that you belong to the number of those who speak this "*me*." Christ did not love only Peter and Paul and give Himself for them, but the same grace belongs and comes to us as to them; therefore we are included in this "*me*." For just as we cannot deny that we are all sinners, and just as we are obliged to say that through his sin Adam destroyed us and made us enemies of God who are liable to God's wrath and judgment and worthy of eternal death—for all terrified hearts feel and confess this, in fact, more than is proper—so we cannot deny that Christ died for our sins in order that we might be justified. For He did not die to make the righteous righteous; He died to make sinners into righteous men, the friends and sons of God, and heirs of all heavenly gifts. Therefore since I feel and confess that I am a sinner on account of the transgression of Adam, why should I not say that I am righteous on account of the righteousness of Christ, especially when I hear that He loved me and gave Himself for me? Paul believed this most firmly, and therefore he speaks with such πληροφορία.[48]

## Notes

1. The phrase *ex opere operato* may simply mean that the validity of a sacrament depends on its proper administration in accordance with the institution of Christ rather than on the holiness of the officiant; in this sense Luther followed and accepted the Augustinian tradition. But in the later Middle Ages it had come to mean an almost automatic or even magical quality in the sacramental act, and it is against this interpretation that Luther is speaking here.

2. [[See page 121 of original . . .—Eds.]], note 37, on these "others."

3. Cf. *Luther's Works*, 2, p. 160.

4. See, among other places, *Luther's Works*, 2, p. 123.

5. Cf. *Luther's Works*, 13, p. 6, note 4.

6. "Habits are qualities or forms adhering to a power *[formae inhaerentes potentiae]*." Thomas Aquinas, *Summa Theologica*, I—II, Q. 54, Art. 1.

7. Cf. Thomas Aquinas, *Summa Theologica*, I—II, Q. 111, Art. 1.

8. See the passages from Duns Scotus quoted by Parthenius Minges, *Ioannis Duns Scoti doctrina philosophica et theologica* (Quaracchi, 1930), I, 506, and II, 444—445.

9. Cf. Thomas Aquinas, *Summa Theologica*, I—II, Q. 109, Arts. 3—4.

10. Where the Weimar text has *praecipientes*, we have read *praecipientis*.

11. Luther uses the Greek word μονόγραμμα here.

12. [[See page 113 of original . . .—Eds.]], note 32.

13. For the Latin *deacceptare* we have used the rare and obsolete English word "disaccept," to retain the contrast with *acceptare* in the original.

14. [[See page 4 of original . . .—Eds.]], note 1.

15. Luther is referring to the following passages: Rom. 6:16; Gal. 3:22; Rom. 3:23.

16. See *Luther's Works*, 22, p. 459, note 156, on this idea.

17. The phrase *sic itur ad astra*, from Vergil, *Aeneid*, IX, 641, had become a common saying.

18. See the Confutation of the Augsburg Confession in M. Reu, *The Augsburg Confession* (Chicago, 1930), II, 352.

19. Cf. Aristotle, *Prior Analytics,* Book II, ch. 23.

20. For the Latin *solarii,* used by Luther's detractors, we have borrowed the Wesleyan term "solafideists."

21. This is one of the passages in the commentary where we may still hear an echo of Luther's lectures.

22. The unusual Latin phrase was *non omnis caro.*

23. Cf. *Luther the Expositor,* p. 150.

24. Cf. Aristotle, *Prior Analytics,* Book II, ch. 17.

25. The Latin words which we have rendered as "denotation" and "connotation" are *res* and *nomen.*

26. Cf. *Luther's Works,* 23, pp. 202–203.

27. Luther frequently links Luke 10:28 with Matt. 19:17; for example, in *Luther's Works,* 22, p. 425.

28. [[See page 138 of original . . .—Eds.]].

29. [[See page 141 of original . . .—Eds.]].

30. The saying, *appellant Scapham scapham,* appears also in *Luther's Works,* 1, p. 5, note 10.

31. Luther's Latin had *minister peccati,* which is reflected in the translation of the Authorized Version, "minister of sin"; but the translation "agent of sin" in the Revised Standard Version renders both the Greek New Testament and Luther's Latin more accurately.

32. On this idea see also *Luther's Works,* 3, p. 8, note 7.

33. This story appears in the *Vitae patrum,* Book III, par. 161, *Patrologia, Series Latina,* LXXIII, 793.

34. [[See page 73 of original . . .—Eds.]], note 53.

35. That is, Christ, not charity, is the *forma* of faith; cf. [[See page 88 of original . . .—Eds.]], note 7.

36. The Weimar text has *fuisses* here, but we have read *fuisset.*

37. [[See page 162 of original . . .—Eds.]], note 81.

38. The original text has the meaningless word *antipophoras;* we have followed the suggestion of the St. Louis edition and read *anthypophora,* a technical term from rhetoric; see, for example, Quintilian, *Institutiones rhetoricae,* IX, 2, 106.

39. The terms are *naturalis vel animalis* and *aliena,* soil, *vita.*

40. [[See page 174 of original . . .—Eds.]] and [[See page 4 of original . . .—Eds.]].

41. On this statement cf. Heiko A. Oberman, *Facientibus quod in se est Deus non denegat gratiam, The Harvard Theological Review*, LV (1962), pp. 317–342.

42. In Latin the verse reads:
*Ultra posse viri*
*Non vult Deus ulla requiri.*
The German text reads:
*Gott fordert nicht von einem Man,*
*Das er mehr thun soll denn er kan.*

43. For *maiorum* in the original we have read *maiorem*.

44. [[See page 132 of original . . .—Eds.]].

45. Although the original reads *Ergo peccator*, etc., the reading *Ego* seems preferable.

46. [[See page 138 of original . . .—Eds.]], this is an echo of Luther's lecture hall.

47. In the original text the words we have printed in italics appear in capitals.

48. Luther uses the Greek word πληροφορία here, perhaps in an allusion to 1 Thess. 1:5.

# The Freedom of a Christian

## Letter of Dedication to Mayor Mühlphordt

To the learned and wise gentleman, Hieronymus Mühlphordt,[1] mayor of Zwickau, my exceptionally gracious friend and patron, I, Martin Luther, Augustinian, present my compliments and good wishes.

My learned and wise sir and gracious friend, the venerable Master Johann Egran, your praiseworthy preacher, spoke to me in terms of praise concerning your love for and pleasure in the Holy Scripture, which you also diligently confess and unceasingly praise before all men. For this reason he desired to make me acquainted with you. I yielded willingly and gladly to his persuasion, for it is a special pleasure to hear of someone who loves divine truth. Unfortunately there are many people, especially those who are proud of their titles, who oppose the truth with all their power and cunning. Admittedly it must be that Christ, set as a stumbling block and a sign that is spoken against, will be an offense and a cause for the fall and rising of many [I Cor. 1:23; Luke 2:34].

In order to make a good beginning of our acquaintance and friendship, I have wished to dedicate to you this treatise or discourse in German, which I have already dedicated to the people in Latin, in the hope that my teachings and writings concerning the papacy will not be considered objectionable by anybody. I commend myself to you and to the grace of God. Amen. Wittenberg, 1520.[2]

## An Open Letter to Pope Leo X

*To Leo X, Pope at Rome, Martin Luther wishes salvation in Christ Jesus our Lord. Amen.* Living among the monsters of this age with whom I am now for the third year waging war, I am compelled occasionally to look up to you, Leo, most blessed father, and to think of you. Indeed, since you are occasionally regarded as the sole cause of my warfare, I cannot help thinking of you. To be sure, the undeserved raging of your godless flatterers against me has compelled me to appeal from your see to a future council, despite the decrees of your predecessors Pins and Julius, who with a foolish tyranny forbade such an appeal. Nevertheless, I have never alienated myself from Your Blessedness to such an extent that I should not with all my heart wish you and your see every blessing, for which I have besought God with earnest prayers to the best of my ability. It is true that I have been so bold as to despise and look down upon those who have tried to frighten me with the majesty of your name and authority. There is one thing, however, which I cannot ignore and which is the cause of my writing once more to Your Blessedness. It has come to my attention that I am accused of great indiscretion, said to be my great fault, in which, it is said, I have not spared even your person.

I freely vow that I have, to my knowledge, spoken only good and honorable words concerning you whenever I have

thought of you. If I had ever done otherwise, I myself could
by no means condone it, but should agree entirely with the
judgment which others have formed of me; and I should do
nothing more gladly than recant such indiscretion and impiety.
I have called you a Daniel in Babylon; and everyone who
reads what I have written knows how zealously I defended
your innocence against your defamer Sylvester.[3] Indeed, your
reputation and the fame of your blameless life, celebrated as
they are throughout the world by the writings of many great
men, are too well known and too honorable to be assailed by
anyone, no matter how great he is. I am not so foolish as to
attack one whom all people praise. As a matter of fact, I have
always tried, and will always continue, not to attack even those
whom the public dishonors for I take no pleasure in the faults
of any man, since I am conscious of the beam in my own eye.
I could not, indeed, be the first one to cast a stone at the adul-
teress [John 8:1–11].

I have, to be sure, sharply attacked ungodly doctrines in
general, and I have snapped at my opponents, not because of
their bad morals, but because of their ungodliness. Rather
than repent this in the least, I have determined to persist in
that fervent zeal and to despise the judgment of men, following
the example of Christ who in his zeal called his opponents "a
brood of vipers," "blind fools," "hypocrites," "children of the
devil" [Matt. 23:13, 17, 33; John 8:44]. Paul branded Magus
[Elymas, the magician] as the "son of the devil, . . . full of all
deceit and villainy" [Acts 13:10], and he calls others "dogs,"
"deceivers," and "adulterers" [Phil 3:2; II Cor. 11:13; 2:17].
If you will allow people with sensitive feelings to judge, they
would consider no person more stinging and unrestrained in
his denunciations than Paul. Who is more stinging than the
prophets? Nowadays, it is true, we are made so sensitive by
the raving crowd of flatterers that we cry out that we are
stung as soon as we meet with disapproval. When we cannot
ward off the truth with any other pretext, we flee from it by
ascribing it to a fierce temper, impatience, and immodesty.

What is the good of salt if it does not bite? Of what use is the edge of a sword if it does not cut? "Cursed is he who does the work of the Lord deceitfully . . ." [Jer. 48:10].

Therefore, most excellent Leo, I beg you to give me a hearing after I have vindicated myself by this letter, and believe me when I say that I have never thought ill of you personally, that I am the kind of a person who would wish you all good things eternally, and that I have no quarrel with any man concerning his morals but only concerning the word of truth. In all other matters I will yield to any man whatsoever; but I have neither the power nor the will to deny the Word of God. If any man has a different opinion concerning me, he does not think straight or understand what I have actually said.

I have truly despised your see, the Roman Curia, which, however, neither you nor anyone else can deny is more corrupt than any Babylon or Sodom ever was, and which, as far as I can see, is characterized by a completely depraved, hopeless, and notorious godlessness. I have been thoroughly incensed over the fact that good Christians are mocked in your name and under the cloak of the Roman church I have resisted and will continue to resist your see as long as the spirit of faith lives in me. Not that I shall strive for the impossible or hope that by my efforts alone anything will be accomplished in that most disordered Babylon, where the fury of so many flatterers is turned against me; but I acknowledge my indebtedness to my Christian brethren, whom I am duty-bound to warn so that fewer of them may be destroyed by the plagues of Rome, at least so that their destruction may be less cruel.

As you well know, there has been flowing from Rome these many years—like a flood covering the world—nothing but a devastation of men's bodies and souls and possessions, the worst examples of the worst of all things. All this is clearer than day to all, and the Roman church, once the holiest of all, has become the most licentious den of thieves [Matt. 21:13], the most shameless of all brothels, the kingdom of sin, death, and hell. It is so bad that even Antichrist himself, if he should come, could think of nothing to add to its wickedness.

Meanwhile you, Leo, sit as a lamb in the midst of wolves [Matt. 10:16] and like Daniel in the midst of lions [Dan. 6:16]. With Ezekiel you live among scorpions [Ezek. 2:6]. How can you alone oppose these monsters? Even if you would call to your aid three or four well learned and thoroughly reliable cardinals, what are these among so many? You would all be poisoned[4] before you could begin to issue a decree for the purpose of remedying the situation. The Roman Curia is already lost, for God's wrath has relentlessly fallen upon it. It detests church councils, it fears a reformation, it cannot allay its own corruption; and what was said of its mother Babylon also applies to it: "We would have cured Babylon, but she was not healed. Let us forsake her" [Jer. 51:9].

It was your duty and that of your cardinals to remedy these evils, but the gout of these evils makes a mockery of the healing hand, and neither chariot nor horse responds to the rein [Virgil, *Georgics* i. 514]. Moved by this affection for you, I have always been sorry, most excellent Leo, that you were made pope in these times, for you are worthy of being pope in better days. The Roman Curia does not deserve to have you or men like you, but it should have Satan himself as pope, for he now actually rules in that Babylon more than you do.

Would that you might discard that which your most profligate enemies boastfully claim to be your glory and might live on a small priestly income of your own or on your family inheritance! No persons are worthy of glorying in that honor except the Iscariots, the sons of perdition. What do you accomplish in the Roman Curia, my Leo? The more criminal and detestable a man is, the more gladly will he use your name to destroy men's possessions and souls, to increase crime, to suppress faith and truth and God's whole church. O most unhappy Leo, you are sitting on a most dangerous throne. I am telling you the truth because I wish you well.

If Bernard felt sorry for Eugenius[5] at a time when the Roman See, which, although even then very corrupt, was ruled with better prospects for improvement, why should not we complain who for three hundred years have had such a great increase of corruption and wickedness? Is it not true that under the vast expanse of heaven there is nothing more corrupt, more pestilential, more offensive than the Roman Curia? It surpasses beyond all comparison the godlessness of the Turks so that, indeed, although it was once a gate of heaven, it is now an open mouth of hell, such a mouth that it cannot be shut because of the wrath of God. Only one thing can we try to do, as I have said:[6] we may be able to call back a few from that yawning chasm of Borne and save them.

Now you see, my Father Leo, how and why I have so violently attacked that pestilential see. So far have I been from raving against your person that I even hoped I might gain your favor and save you if I should make a strong and stinging assault upon that prison, that veritable hell of yours. For you and your salvation and the salvation of many others with you will be served by everything that men of ability can do against the confusion of this wicked Curia. They serve your office who do every harm to the Curia; they glorify Christ who in every way curse it. In short, they are Christians who are not Romans.

To enlarge upon this, I never intended to attack the Roman Curia or to raise any controversy concerning it. But when I saw all efforts to save it were hopeless, I despised it, gave it a bill of divorce [Deut. 24:1], and said, "Let the evildoer still do evil, and the filthy still be filthy" [Rev. 22:11]. Then I turned to the quiet and peaceful study of the Holy Scriptures so that I might be helpful to my brothers around me. When I had made some progress in these studies, Satan opened his eyes and then filled his servant Johann Eck, a notable enemy of Christ, with an insatiable lust for glory and thus aroused him to drag me unawares to a debate, seizing me by means of one little word which I had let slip concerning the primacy of the

Roman church. Then that boastful braggart,[7] frothing and gnashing his teeth, declared that he would risk everything for the glory of God and the honor of the Apostolic See. Puffed up with the prospect of abusing your authority, he looked forward with great confidence to a victory over me. He was concerned not so much with establishing the primacy of Peter as he was with demonstrating his own leadership among the theologians of our time. To that end he considered it no small advantage to triumph over Luther. When the debate ended badly for the sophist, an unbelievable madness overcame the man, for he believed that it was his fault alone which was responsible for my disclosing all the infamy of Rome.

Allow me, I pray, most excellent Leo, this once to plead my cause and to indict your real enemies. You know, I believe, what dealings your legate, cardinal of St. Sisto,[8] an unwise and unfortunate, or rather, an unreliable man, had with me. When out of reverence for your name I had placed myself and my cause in his hands, he did not try to establish peace. He could easily have done so with a single word, for at that time I promised to keep silent and to end the controversy, provided my opponents were ordered to do likewise. As he was a man who sought glory, however, and was not content with such an agreement, he began to defend my opponents, to give them full freedom, and to order me to recant, even though this was not included in his instructions. When matters went fairly well, he with his churlish arbitrariness made them far worse. Therefore Luther is not to blame for what followed. All the blame is Cajetan's, who did not permit me to keep silent, as I at that time most earnestly requested him to do. What more should I have done?

There followed Karl Miltitz,[9] also a nuncio of Your Holiness, who exerted much effort and traveled back and forth, omitting nothing that might help restore the order which Cajetan had rashly and arrogantly disturbed. He finally, with the help of the most illustrious prince, the Elector Frederick, managed to arrange several private conferences with me.[10]

Again I yielded out of respect for your name, was prepared to keep silent, and even accepted as arbiter either the archbishop of Trier or the bishop of Naumburg. So matters were arranged. But while this arrangement was being followed with good prospects of success, behold, that other and greater enemy of yours, Eck, broke in with the Leipzig Debate which he had undertaken against Dr. Karlstadt. When the new question of the primacy of the pope was raised, he suddenly turned his weapons against me and completely upset our arrangement for maintaining peace. Meanwhile Karl Miltitz waited. The debate was held and judges were selected. But again no decision was reached, which is not surprising, for through Eck's lies, tricks, and wiles everything was stirred up, aggravated, and confused worse than ever. Regardless of the decision which might have been reached, a greater conflagration would have resulted, for he sought glory, not the truth. Again I left undone nothing that I ought to have done.

I admit that on this occasion no small amount of corrupt Roman practices came to light, but whatever wrong was done was Eck's fault, who undertook a task beyond his capacities. Striving insanely for his own glory, he revealed the shame of Rome to all the world. This man is your enemy, my dear Leo, or rather the enemy of your Curia. From his example alone we can learn that no enemy is more pernicious than a flatterer. What did he accomplish with his flattery but an evil which not even a king could have accomplished? The name of the Roman Curia is today a stench throughout the world, papal authority languishes, and Roman ignorance, once honored, is in ill repute. We should have heard nothing of all this if Eck had not upset the peace arrangements made by Karl [von Miltitz] and myself. Eck himself now clearly sees this and, although it is too late and to no avail, he is furious that my books were published. He should have thought of this when, like a whinnying horse, he was madly seeking his own glory and preferred his own advantage through you and at the greatest peril to you. The vain man thought that I would stop and keep silent out of fear for your name, for I do not believe that he entirely trusted his cleverness and learning. Now that he sees that I have more courage than that and have not been silenced, he repents of his rashness, but too late, and perceives—if indeed he does finally understand—that there is One in heaven who opposes the proud and humbles the haughty [I Pet. 5:5; Jth. 6:15].

Since we gained nothing from this debate except greater confusion to the Roman cause, Karl Miltitz, in a third attempt to bring about peace, came to the fathers of the Augustinian Order assembled in their chapter and sought their advice in settling the controversy which had now grown most disturbing and dangerous. Because, by God's favor, they had no hope of proceeding against me by violent means, some of their most famous men were sent to me. These men asked me at least to show honor to the person of Your Blessedness and in a humble letter to plead as my excuse your innocence and mine in the matter. They said that the affair was not yet in a hopeless state, provided Leo X out of his innate goodness would take a hand in it. As I have always both offered and desired peace so that I might devote myself to quieter and more useful studies, and have stormed with such great fury merely for the purpose of overwhelming my unequal opponents by the volume and violence of words no less than of intellect, I not only gladly ceased but also joyfully and thankfully considered this suggestion a very welcome kindness to me, provided our hope could be realized.

So I come, most blessed father, and, prostrate before you, pray that if possible you intervene and stop those flatterers, who are the enemies of peace while they pretend to keep peace. But let no person imagine that I will recant unless he prefer to involve the whole question in even greater turmoil. Furthermore, I acknowledge no fixed rules for the interpretation of the Word of God, since the Word of God, which teaches freedom in all other matters, must not be bound [II Tim. 2:9]. If these two points are granted, there is nothing that I could not or would not most willingly do or endure. I detest contentions. I will challenge no one. On the other hand, I do not want others to challenge me. If they do, as Christ is my teacher, I will not be speechless. When once this controversy has been cited before you and settled, Your Blessedness will be able with a brief and ready word to silence both parties and command them to keep the peace. That is what I have always wished to hear.

Therefore, my Father Leo, do not listen to those sirens who pretend that you are no mere man but a demigod so that you may command and require whatever you wish. It will not be done in that manner and you will not have such remarkable power. You are a servant of servants,[11] and more than all other men you are in a most miserable and dangerous position. Be not deceived by those who pretend that you are lord of the world, allow no one to be considered a Christian unless he accepts your authority, and prate that you have power over heaven, hell, and purgatory. These men are your enemies who seek to destroy your soul [I Kings 19:10], as Isaiah says: "O my people, they that call thee blessed, the same deceive thee" [Isa. 3:12]. They err who exalt you above a council and the church universal. They err who ascribe to you alone the right of interpreting Scripture. Under the protection of your name they seek to gain support for all their wicked deeds in the church. Alas! Through them Satan has already made much progress under your predecessors. In short, believe none who exalt you, believe those who humble you. This is the judgment of God, that ". . . he has put down the mighty from their thrones and exalted those of low degree" [Luke 1:52]. See how different Christ is from his successors, although they all would wish to be his vicars. I fear that most of them have been too literally his vicars. A man is a vicar only when his superior is absent. If the pope rules, while Christ is absent and does not dwell in his heart, what else is he but a vicar of Christ? What is the church under such a vicar but a mass of people without Christ? Indeed, what is such a vicar but an antichrist and an idol? How much more properly did the apostles call themselves servants of the present Christ and not vicars of an absent Christ?

Perhaps I am presumptuous in trying to instruct so exalted a personage from whom we all should learn and from whom the thrones of judges receive their decisions, as those pestilential fellows of yours boast. But I am following the example of St. Bernard in his book, *On Consideration*,[12] to Pope Eugenius, a book every pope should know from memory. I follow him, not because I am eager to instruct you, but out of pure and loyal concern which compels us to be interested in all the affairs of our neighbors, even when they are protected, and which does not permit us to take into consideration either their dignity or lack of dignity since it is only concerned with the dangers they face or the advantages they may gain. I know that Your Blessedness is driven and buffeted about in Home, that is, that far out at sea you are threatened on all sides by dangers and are working very hard in the miserable situation so that you are in need of even the slightest help of the least of your brothers. Therefore I do not consider it absurd if I now forget your exalted office and do what brotherly love demands. I have no desire to flatter you in so serious and dangerous a matter. If men do not perceive that I am your friend and your most humble subject in this matter, there is One who understands and judges [John 8:50].

Finally, that I may not approach you empty-handed, blessed father, I am sending you this little treatise[13] dedicated to you as a token of peace and good hope. From this book you may judge with what studies I should prefer to be more profitably occupied, as I could be, provided your godless flatterers would permit me and had permitted me in the past. It is a small book if you regard its size. Unless I am mistaken, however, it contains the whole of Christian life in a brief form, provided you grasp its meaning. I am a poor man and have no other gift to offer, and you do not need to be enriched by any but a spiritual gift. May the Lord Jesus preserve you forever. Amen. Wittenberg, September 6, 1520.

## Martin Luther's Treatise on Christian Liberty [The Freedom of a Christian]

Many people have considered Christian faith an easy thing, and not a few have given it a place among the virtues. They do this because they have not experienced it and have never tasted the great strength there is in faith. It is impossible to write well about it or to understand what has been written about it unless one has at one time or another experienced the courage which faith gives a man when trials oppress him. But he who has had even a faint taste of it can never write, speak, meditate, or hear enough concerning it. It is a living "spring of water welling up to eternal life," as Christ calls it in John 4[:14].

As for me, although I have no wealth of faith to boast of and know how scant my supply is, I nevertheless hope that I have attained to a little faith, even though I have been assailed by great and various temptations; and I hope that I can discuss it, if not more elegantly, certainly more to the point, than those literalists and subtle disputants have previously done, who have not even understood what they have written.

To make the way smoother for the unlearned—for only them do I serve—I shall set down the following two propositions concerning the freedom and the bondage of the spirit:

A Christian is a perfectly free lord of all, subject
   to none.
A Christian is a perfectly dutiful servant of all,
   subject to all.

These two theses seem to contradict each other. If, however, they should be found to fit together they would serve our purpose beautifully. Both are Paul's own statements, who says in I Cor. 9[:19], "For though I am free [from] all men, I have made myself a slave to all," and in Rom. 13[:8], "Owe no one anything, except to love one another." Love by its very nature is ready to serve and be subject to him who is loved. So Christ, although he was Lord of all, was "born of woman, born under the law" [Gal. 4:4], and therefore was at the same time a free man and a servant, "in the form of God" and "of a servant" [Phil. 2:6–7].

Let us start, however, with something more remote from our subject, but more obvious. Man has a twofold nature, a spiritual and a bodily one. According to the spiritual nature, which men refer to as the soul, he is called a spiritual, inner, or new man. According to the bodily nature, which men refer to as flesh, he is called a carnal, outward, or old man, of whom the Apostle writes in II Cor. 4[:16], "Though our outer nature is wasting away, our inner nature is being renewed every day." Because of this diversity of nature the Scriptures assert contradictory things concerning the same man, since these two men in the same man contradict each other, "for the desires of the flesh are against the Spirit, and the desires of the Spirit are against the flesh," according to Gal. 5[:17].

First, let us consider the inner man to see how a righteous, free, and pious Christian, that is, a spiritual, new, and inner man, becomes what he is. It is evident that no external thing has any influence in producing Christian righteousness or freedom, or in producing unrighteousness or servitude. A simple argument will furnish the proof of this statement. What can it profit the soul if the body is well, free, and active, and eats, drinks, and does as it pleases? For in these respects even the most godless slaves of vice may prosper. On the other hand, how will poor health or imprisonment or hunger or thirst or any other external misfortune harm the soul? Even the most godly men, and those who are free because of clear consciences, are afflicted with these things. None of these things touch either the freedom or the servitude of the soul. It does not help the soul if the body is adorned with the sacred robes of priests or dwells in sacred places or is occupied with sacred duties or prays, fasts, abstains from certain kinds of food, or does any work that can be done by the body and in the body. The righteousness and the freedom of the soul require something far different since the things which have been mentioned could be done by any wicked person. Such works produce nothing but hypocrites. On the other hand, it will not harm the soul if the body is clothed in secular dress, dwells in unconsecrated places, eats and drinks as others do, does not pray aloud, and neglects to do all the above-mentioned things which hypocrites can do.

Furthermore, to put aside all kinds of works, even contemplation, meditation, and all that the soul can do, does not help. One thing, and only one thing, is necessary for Christian life, righteousness, and freedom. That one thing is the most holy Word of God, the gospel of Christ, as Christ says, John 11[:25], "I am the resurrection and the life; he who believes in me, though he die, yet shall he live"; and John 8[:36], "So if the Son makes you free, you will be free indeed"; and Matt. 4[:4], "Man shall not live by bread alone, but by every word that proceeds from the mouth of God." Let us then consider it certain and firmly established that the soul can do without anything except the Word of God and that where the Word of God is missing there is no help at all for the soul. If it has the Word of God it is rich and lacks nothing since it is the Word of life, truth, light, peace, righteousness, salvation, joy, liberty, wisdom, power, grace, glory, and of every incalculable blessing. This is why the prophet in the entire Psalm [119] and in many other places yearns and sighs for the Word of God and uses so many names to describe it.

On the other hand, there is no more terrible disaster with which the wrath of God can afflict men than a famine of the hearing of his Word, as he says in Amos [8:11]. Likewise there is no greater mercy than when he sends forth his Word, as we read in Psalm 107[:20]: "He sent forth his word, and healed them, and delivered them from destruction." Nor was

Christ sent into the world for any other ministry except that of the Word. Moreover, the entire spiritual estate—all the apostles, bishops, and priests—has been called and instituted only for the ministry of the Word.

You may ask, "What then is the Word of God, and how shall it be used, since there are so many words of God?" I answer: The Apostle explains this in Romans 1. The Word is the gospel of God concerning his Son, who was made flesh, suffered, rose from the dead, and was glorified through the Spirit who sanctifies. To preach Christ means to feed the soul, make it righteous, set it free, and save it, provided it believes the preaching. Faith alone is the saving and efficacious use of the Word of God, according to Rom. 10[:9]: "If you confess with your lips that Jesus is Lord and believe in your heart that God raised him from the dead, you will be saved." Furthermore, "Christ is the end of the law, that everyone who has faith may be justified" [Rom. 10:4]. Again, in Rom. 1[:17], "He who through faith is righteous shall live." The Word of God cannot be received and cherished by any works whatever but only by faith. Therefore it is clear that, as the soul needs only the Word of God for its life and righteousness, so it is justified by faith alone and not any works; for if it could be justified by anything else, it would not need the Word, and consequently it would not need faith.

This faith cannot exist in connection with works—that is to say, if you at the same time claim to be justified by works, whatever their character—for that would be the same as "limping with two different opinions" [I Kings 18:21], as worshiping Baal and kissing one's own hand [Job 31:27–28], which, as Job says, is a very great iniquity. Therefore the moment you begin to have faith you learn that all things in you are altogether blameworthy, sinful, and damnable, as the Apostle says in Rom. 3[:23], "Since all have sinned and fall short of the glory of God," and, "None is righteous, no, not one; . . . all have turned aside, together they have gone wrong" (Rom. 3:10–12). When you have learned this you will know that you need Christ, who suffered and rose again for you so that, if you believe in him, you may through this faith become a new man in so far as your sins are forgiven and you are justified by the merits of another, namely, of Christ alone.

Since, therefore, this faith can rule only in the inner man, as Rom. 10[:10] says, "For man believes with his heart and so is justified," and since faith alone justifies, it is clear that the inner man cannot be justified, freed, or saved by any outer work or action at all, and that these works, whatever their character, have nothing to do with this inner man. On the other hand, only ungodliness and unbelief of heart, and no outer work, make him guilty and a damnable servant of sin. Wherefore it ought to be the first concern of every Christian to lay aside all confidence in works and increasingly to strengthen faith alone and through faith to grow in the knowledge, not of works, but of Christ Jesus, who suffered and rose for him, as Peter teaches in the last chapter of his first Epistle (I Pet. 5:10). No other work makes a Christian. Thus when the Jews asked Christ, as related in John 6[:28], what they must do "to be doing the work of God," he brushed aside the multitude of works which he saw they did in great profusion and suggested one work, saying, "This is the work of God, that you believe in him whom he has sent" [John 6:29]; "for on him has God the Father set his seal" [John 6:27].

Therefore true faith in Christ is a treasure beyond comparison which brings with it complete salvation and saves man from every evil, as Christ says in the last chapter of Mark [16:16]: "He who believes and is baptized will be saved; but he who does not believe will be condemned." Isaiah contemplated this treasure and foretold it in chapter 10: "The Lord will make a small and consuming word upon the land, and it will overflow with righteousness" [Cf. Isa. 10:22]. This is as though he said, "Faith, which is a small and perfect fulfilment of the law, will fill believers with so great a righteousness that they will need nothing more to become righteous." So

Paul says, Rom. 10[:10], "For man believes with his heart and so is justified."

Should you ask how it happens that faith alone justifies and offers us such a treasure of great benefits without works in view of the fact that so many works, ceremonies, and laws are prescribed in the Scriptures, I answer: First of all, remember what has been said, namely, that faith alone, without works, justifies, frees, and saves; we shall make this clearer later on. Here we must point out that the entire Scripture of God is divided into two parts: commandments and promises. Although the commandments teach things that are good, the things taught are not done as soon as they are taught, for the commandments show us what we ought to do but do not give us the power to do it. They are intended to teach man to know himself, that through them he may recognize his inability to do good and may despair of his own ability. That is why they are called the Old Testament and constitute the Old Testament. For example, the commandment, "You shall not covet" [Exod. 20:17], is a command which proves us all to be sinners, for no one can avoid coveting no matter how much he may struggle against it. Therefore, in order not to covet and to fulfil the commandment, a man is compelled to despair of himself, to seek the help which he does not find in himself elsewhere and from someone else, as stated in Hosea [13:9]: "Destruction is your own, O Israel: your help is only in me." As we fare with respect to one commandment, so we fare with all, for it is equally impossible for us to keep any one of them.

Now when a man has learned through the commandments to recognize his helplessness and is distressed about how he might satisfy the law—since the law must be fulfilled so that not a jot or tittle shall be lost, otherwise man will be condemned without hope—then, being truly humbled and reduced to nothing in his own eyes, he finds in himself nothing whereby he may be justified and saved. Here the second part of Scripture comes to our aid, namely, the promises of God which declare the glory of God, saying, "If you wish to fulfil the law and not covet, as the law demands, come, believe in Christ in whom grace, righteousness, peace, liberty, and all things are promised you. If you believe, you shall have all things; if you do not believe, you shall lack all things." That which is impossible for you to accomplish by trying to fulfil all the works of the law—many and useless as they all are— you will accomplish quickly and easily through faith. God our Father has made all things depend on faith so that whoever has faith will have everything, and whoever does not have faith will have nothing. "For God has consigned all men to disobedience, that he may have mercy upon all," as it is stated in Rom. 11[:32]. Thus the promises of God give what the commandments of God demand and fulfil what the law prescribes so that all things may be Coifs alone, both the commandments and the fulfilling of the commandments. He alone commands, he alone fulfils. Therefore the promises of God belong to the New Testament. Indeed, they are the New Testament.

Since these promises of God are holy, true, righteous, free, and peaceful words, full of goodness, the soul which clings to them with a firm faith will be so closely united with them and altogether absorbed by them that it not only will share in all their power but will be saturated and intoxicated by them. If a touch of Christ healed, how much more will this most tender spiritual touch, this absorbing of the Word, communicate to the soul all things that belong to the Word.

This, then, is how through faith alone without works the soul is justified by the Word of God, sanctified, made true, peaceful, and free, filled with every blessing and truly made a child of God, as John 1[:12] says: "But to all who . . . believed in his name, he gave power to become children of God."

From what has been said it is easy to see from what source faith derives such great power and why a good work or all good works together cannot equal it. No good work can rely upon the Word of God or live in the soul, for faith alone and the Word of God rule in the soul. Just as the heated iron glows like fire because of the union of fire with it, so the Word imparts its qualities to the soul. It is clear, then, that a Christian has all that he needs in faith and needs no works to justify him; and if he has no need of works, he has no need of the law; and if he has no need of the law, surely he is free from the law. It is true that "the law is not laid down for the just" [I Tim. 1:9]. This is that Christian liberty, our faith, which does not induce us to live in idleness or wickedness but makes the law and works unnecessary for any man's righteousness and salvation.

This is the first power of faith. Let us now examine also the second. It is a further function of faith that it honors him whom it trusts with the most reverent and highest regard since it considers him truthful and trustworthy. There is no other honor equal to the estimate of truthfulness and righteousness with which we honor him whom we trust. Could we ascribe to a man anything greater than truthfulness and righteousness and perfect goodness? On the other hand, there is no way in which we can show greater contempt for a man than to regard him as false and wicked and to be suspicious of him, as we do when we do not trust him. So when the soul firmly trusts God's promises, it regards him as truthful and righteous. Nothing more excellent than this can be ascribed to God. The very highest worship of God is this that we ascribe to him truthfulness, righteousness, and whatever else should be ascribed to one who is trusted. When this is done, the soul consents to his will. Then it hallows his name and allows itself to be treated according to God's good pleasure for, clinging to God's promises, it does not doubt that he who is true, just, and wise will do, dispose, and provide all things well.

Is not such a soul most obedient to God in all things by this faith? What commandment is there that such obedience has not completely fulfilled? What more complete fulfilment is there than obedience in all things? This obedience, however, is not rendered by works, but by faith alone. On the other hand, what greater rebellion against God, what greater wickedness, what greater contempt of God is there than not believing his promise? For what is this but to make God a liar or to doubt that he is truthful?—that is, to ascribe truthfulness to one's self but lying and vanity to God? Does not a man who does this deny God and set himself up as an idol in his heart? Then of what good are works done in such wickedness, even if they were the works of angels and apostles? Therefore God has rightly included all things, not under anger or lust, but under unbelief, so that they who imagine that they are fulfilling the law by doing the works of chastity and mercy required by the law (the civil and human virtues) might not be saved. They are included under the sin of unbelief and must either seek mercy or be justly condemned.

When, however, God sees that we consider him truth and by the faith of our heart pay him the great honor which is due him, he does us that great honor of considering us truthful and righteous for the sake of our faith. Faith works truth and righteousness by giving God what belongs to him. Therefore God in turn glorifies our righteousness. It is true and just that God is truthful and just, and to consider and confess him to be so is the same as being truthful and just. Accordingly he says in I Sam. 2[:30], "Those who honor me I will honor, and those who despise me shall be lightly esteemed." So Paul says in Rom. 4[:3] that Abraham's faith "was reckoned to him as righteousness" because by it he gave glory most perfectly to God, and that for the same reason our faith shall be reckoned to us as righteousness if we believe.

The third incomparable benefit of faith is that it unites the soul with Christ as a bride is united with her bridegroom. By this mystery, as the Apostle teaches, Christ and the soul become one flesh [Eph. 5:31–32]. And if they are one flesh and there is between them a true marriage—indeed the most perfect of all marriages, since human marriages are but poor examples of this one true marriage—it follows that everything they have they hold in common, the good as well as the evil.

Accordingly the believing soul can boast of and glory in whatever Christ has as though it were its own, and whatever the soul has Christ claims as his own. Let us compare these and we shall see inestimable benefits. Christ is full of grace, life, and salvation. The soul is full of sins, death, and damnation. Now let faith come between them and sins, death, and damnation will be Christ's, while grace, life, and salvation will be the soul's; for if Christ is a bridegroom, he must take upon himself the things which are his bride's and bestow upon her the things that are his. If he gives her his body and very self, how shall he not give her all that is his? And if he takes the body of the bride, how shall he not take all that is hers?

Here we have a most pleasing vision not only of communion but of a blessed struggle and victory and salvation and redemption. Christ is God and man in one person. He has neither sinned nor died, and is not condemned, and he cannot sin, die, or be condemned; his righteousness, life, and salvation are unconquerable, eternal, omnipotent. By the wedding ring of faith he shares in the sins, death, and pains of hell which are his bride's. As a matter of fact, he makes them his own and acts as if they were his own and as if he himself had sinned; he suffered, died, and descended into hell that he might overcome them all. Now since it was such a one who did all this, and death and hell could not swallow him up, these were necessarily swallowed up by him in a mighty duel; for his righteousness is greater than the sins of all men, his life stronger than death, his salvation more invincible than hell. Thus the believing soul by means of the pledge of its faith is free in Christ, its bridegroom, free from all sins, secure against death and hell, and is endowed with the eternal righteousness, life, and salvation of Christ its bridegroom. So he takes to himself a glorious bride, "without spot or wrinkle, cleansing her by the washing of water with the word" [Cf. Eph. 5:26–27] of life, that is, by faith in the Word of life, righteousness, and salvation. In this way he marries her in faith, steadfast love, and in mercies, righteousness, and justice, as Hos. 2[:19–20] says.

Who then can fully appreciate what this royal marriage means? Who can understand the riches of the glory of this grace? Here this rich and divine bridegroom Christ marries this poor, wicked harlot, redeems her from all her evil, and adorns her with all his goodness. Her sins cannot now destroy her, since they are laid upon Christ and swallowed up by him. And she has that righteousness in Christ, her husband, of which she may boast as of her own and which she can confidently display alongside her sins in the face of death and hell and say, "If I have sinned, yet my Christ, in whom I believe, has not sinned, and all his is mine and all mine is his," as the bride in the Song of Solomon [2:16] says, "My beloved is mine and I am his." This is what Paul means when he says in I Cor. 15[:57], "Thanks be to God, who gives us the victory through our Lord Jesus Christ," that is, the victory over sin and death, as he also says there, "The sting of death is sin, and the power of sin is the law" [I Cor. 15:56].

From this you once more see that much is ascribed to faith, namely, that it alone can fulfil the law and justify without works. You see that the First Commandment, which says, "You shall worship one God," is fulfilled by faith alone. Though you were nothing but good works from the soles of your feet to the crown of your head, you would still not be righteous or worship God or fulfil the First Commandment, since God cannot be worshiped unless you ascribe to him the glory of truthfulness and all goodness which is due him. This cannot be done by works but only by the faith of the heart. Not by the doing of works but by believing do we glorify God and acknowledge that he is truthful. Therefore faith alone is the righteousness of a Christian and the fulfilling of all the commandments, for he who fulfils the First Commandment has no difficulty in fulfilling all the rest.

But works, being inanimate things, cannot glorify God, although they can, if faith is present, be done to the glory of God. Here, however, we are not inquiring what works and what kind of works are done, but who it is that does them, who glorifies God and brings forth the works. This is done by faith which dwells in the heart and is the source and substance of all our righteousness. Therefore it is a blind and dangerous doctrine which teaches that the commandments must be fulfilled by works. The commandments must be fulfilled before any works can be done, and the works proceed from the fulfilment of the commandments [Rom. 13:10], as we shall hear.

That we may examine more profoundly that grace which our inner man has in Christ, we must realize that in the Old Testament God consecrated to himself all the first-born males. The birthright was highly prized for it involved a twofold honor, that of priesthood and that of kingship. The first-born brother was priest and lord over all the others and a type of Christ, the true and only first-born of God the Father and the Virgin Mary and true king and priest, but not after the fashion of the flesh and the world, for his kingdom is not of this world [John 18:36]. He reigns in heavenly and spiritual things and consecrates them—things such as righteousness, truth, wisdom, peace, salvation, etc. This does not mean that all things on earth and in hell are not also subject to him—otherwise how could he protect and save us from them? —but that his kingdom consists neither in them nor of them. Nor does his priesthood consist in the outer splendor of robes and postures like those of the human priesthood of Aaron and our present-day church; but it consists of spiritual things through which he by an invisible service intercedes for us in heaven before God, there offers himself as a sacrifice, and does all things a priest should do, as Paul describes him under the type of Melchizedek in the Epistle to the Hebrews [Heb. 6–7]. Nor does he only pray and intercede for us but he teaches us inwardly through the living instruction of his Spirit, thus performing the two real functions of a priest, of which the prayers and the preaching of human priests are visible types.

Now just as Christ by his birthright obtained these two prerogatives, so he imparts them to and shares them with

everyone who believes in him according to the law of the
above-mentioned marriage, according to which the wife
owns whatever belongs to the husband. Hence all of us who
believe in Christ are priests and kings in Christ, as I Pet.
2[:9] says; "You are a chosen race, God's own people, a royal
priesthood, a priestly kingdom, that you may declare the
wonderful deeds of him who called you out of darkness into
his marvelous light."

The nature of this priesthood and kingship is something
like this: First, with respect to the kingship, every Christian
is by faith so exalted above all things that, by virtue of a
spiritual power, he is lord of all things without exception, so
that nothing can do him any harm. As a matter of fact, all
things are made subject to him and are compelled to serve
him in obtaining salvation. Accordingly Paul says in Rom.
8[:28], "All things work together for good for the elect," and
in I Cor. 3[:21–23], "All things are yours whether . . . life or
death or the present or the future, all are yours; and you are
Christ's. . . ." This is not to say that every Christian is placed
over all things to have and control them by physical power—a
madness with which some churchmen are afflicted—for such
power belongs to kings, princes, and other men on earth. Our
ordinary experience in life shows us that we are subjected to
all, suffer many things, and even die.

As a matter of fact, the more Christian a man is, the more
evils, sufferings, and deaths he must endure, as we see in Christ
the first-born prince himself, and in all his brethren, the saints.
The power of which we speak is spirtual. It rules in the midst
of enemies and is powerful in the midst of oppression. This
means nothing else than that "power is made perfect in weakness" [II Cor. 12:9] and that in all things I can find profit
toward salvation [Rom. 8:28], so that the cross and death
itself are compelled to serve me and to work together with
me for my salvation. This is a splendid privilege and hard to
attain, a truly omnipotent power, a spiritual dominion in
which there is nothing so good and nothing so evil but that

it shall work together for good to me, if only I believe. Yes, since faith alone suffices for salvation, I need nothing except faith exercising the power and dominion of its own liberty. Lo, this is the inestimable power and liberty of Christians.

Not only are we the freest of kings, we are also priests forever, which is far more excellent than being kings, for as priests we are worthy to appear before God to pray for others and to teach one another divine things. These are the functions of priests, and they cannot be granted to any unbeliever. Thus Christ has made it possible for us, provided we believe in him, to be not only his brethren, co-heirs, and fellow-kings, but also his fellow-priests. Therefore we may boldly come into the presence of God in the spirit of faith [Heb. 10:19, 22] and cry "Abba, Father!" pray for one another, and do all things which we see done and foreshadowed in the outer and visible works of priests.

He, however, who does not believe is not served by anything. On the contrary, nothing works for his good, but he himself is a servant of all, and all things turn out badly for him because he wickedly uses them to his own advantage and not to the glory of God. So he is no priest but a wicked man whose prayer becomes sin and who never comes into the presence of God because God does not hear sinners [John 9:31]. Who then can comprehend the lofty dignity of the Christian? By virtue of his royal power he rules over all things, death, life, and sin, and through his priestly glory is omnipotent with God because he does the things which God asks and desires, as it is written, "He will fulfil the desire of those who fear him; he also will hear their cry and save them" [Cf. Phil. 4:13]. To this glory a man attains, certainly not by any works of his, but by faith alone.

From this anyone can clearly see how a Christian is free from all things and over all things so that he needs no works to make him righteous and save him, since faith alone abundantly confers all these things. Should he grow so foolish, however, as to presume to become righteous, free, saved, and a Christian by means of some good work, he would instantly lose faith and all its benefits, a foolishness aptly illustrated in the fable of the dog who runs along a stream with a piece of meat in his mouth and, deceived by the reflection of the meat in the water, opens his mouth to snap at it and so loses both the meat and the reflection.[14]

You will ask, "If all who are in the church are priests, how do these whom we now call priests differ from laymen?" I answer: Injustice is done those words "priest," "cleric," "spiritual," "ecclesiastic," when they are transferred from all Christians to those few who are now by a mischievous usage called "ecclesiastics." Holy Scripture makes no distinction between them, although it gives the name "ministers," "servants," "stewards" to those who are now proudly called popes, bishops, and lords and who should according to the ministry of the Word serve others and teach them the faith of Christ and the freedom of believers. Although we are all equally priests, we cannot all publicly minister and teach. We ought not do so even if we could. Paul writes accordingly in I Cor. 4 [1], "This is how one should regard us, as servants of Christ and stewards of the mysteries of God."

That stewardship, however, has now been developed into so great a display of power and so terrible a tyranny that no heathen empire or other earthly power can be compared with it, just as if laymen were not also Christians. Through this perversion the knowledge of Christian grace, faith, liberty, and of Christ himself has altogether perished, and its place has been taken by an unbearable bondage of human works and laws until we have become, as the Lamentations of Jeremiah [1] say, servants of the vilest men on earth who abuse our misfortune to serve only their base and shameless will.

To return to our purpose, I believe that it has now become clear that it is not enough or in any sense Christian to preach the works, life, and words of Christ as historical facts, as if the knowledge of these would suffice for the conduct of life; yet this is the fashion among those who must today be regarded

as our best preachers. Far less is it sufficient or Christian to
say nothing at all about Christ and to teach instead the laws
of men and the decrees of the fathers. Now there are not a few
who preach Christ and read about him that they may move
men's affections to sympathy with Christ, to anger against the
Jews, and such childish and effeminate nonsense. Rather ought
Christ to be preached to the end that faith in him may be
established that he may not only be Christ, but be Christ for
you and me, and that what is said of him and is denoted in
his name may be effectual in us. Such faith is produced and
preserved in us by preaching why Christ came, what he brought
and bestowed, what benefit it is to us to accept him. This is
done when that Christian liberty which he bestows is rightly
taught and we are told in what way we Christians are all kings
and priests and therefore lords of all and may firmly believe
that whatever we have done is pleasing and acceptable in the
sight of God, as I have already said.

What man is there whose heart, upon hearing these things,
will not rejoice to its depth, and when receiving such comfort
will not grow tender so that he will love Christ as he never
could by means of any laws or works? Who would have the
power to harm or frighten such a heart? If the knowledge of
sin or the fear of death should break in upon it, it is ready to
hope in the Lord. It does not grow afraid when it hears tidings
of evil. It is not disturbed when it sees its enemies. This is so
because it believes that the righteousness of Christ is its own
and that its sin is not its own, but Christ's, and that all sin is
swallowed up by the righteousness of Christ. This, as has been
said above,[15] is a necessary consequence on account of faith
in Christ. So the heart learns to scoff at death and sin and to
say with the Apostle, "O death, where is thy victory? O death,
where is thy sting? The sting of death is sin, and the power
of sin is the law. But thanks be to God, who gives us the
victory through our Lord Jesus Christ" [I Cor. 15:55–57].
Death is swallowed up not only in the victory of Christ but

also by our victory, because through faith his victory has become ours and in that faith we also are conquerors.

Let this suffice concerning the inner man, his liberty, and the source of his liberty, the righteousness of faith. He needs neither laws nor good works but, on the contrary, is injured by them if he believes that he is justified by them.

Now let us turn to the second part, the outer man. Here we shall answer all those who, offended by the word "faith" and by all that has been said, now ask, "If faith does all things and is alone sufficient unto righteousness, why then are good works commanded? We will take our ease and do no works and be content with faith." I answer: not so, you wicked men, not so. That would indeed be proper if we were wholly inner and perfectly spiritual men. But such we shall be only at the last day, the day of the resurrection of the dead. As long as we live in the flesh we only begin to make some progress in that which shall be perfected in the future life. For this reason the Apostle in Rom. 8[:23] calls all that we attain in this life "the first fruits of the Spirit" because we shall indeed receive the greater portion, even the fulness of the Spirit, in the future. This is the place to assert that which was said above, namely, that a Christian is the servant of all and made subject to all. Insofar as he is free he does no works, but insofar as he is a servant he does all kinds of works. How this is possible we shall see.

Although, as I have said, a man is abundantly and sufficiently justified by faith inwardly, in his spirit, and so has all that he needs, except insofar as this faith and these riches must grow from day to day even to the future life; yet he remains in this mortal life on earth. In this life he must control his own body and have dealings with men. Here the works begin; here a man cannot enjoy leisure; here he must indeed take care to discipline his body by fastings, watchings, labors, and other reasonable discipline and to subject it to the Spirit so that it will obey and conform to the inner man and faith and not revolt against faith and hinder the inner man, as it is the nature of the body to do if it is not held in check. The inner man, who by faith is created in the image of God, is both joyful and happy because of Christ in whom so many benefits are conferred upon him; and therefore it is his one occupation to serve God joyfully and without thought of gain, in love that is not constrained.

While he is doing this, behold, he meets a contrary will in his own flesh which strives to serve the world and seeks its own advantage. This the spirit of faith cannot tolerate, but with joyful zeal it attempts to put the body under control and hold it in check, as Paul says in Rom. 7[:22–23], "For I delight in the law of God, in my inmost self, but I see in my members another law at war with the law of my mind and making me captive to the law of sin," and in another place, "But I pommel my body and subdue it, lest after preaching to others I myself should be disqualified" [I Cor. 9:27], and in Galatians [5:24], "And those who belong to Christ Jesus have crucified the flesh with its passions and desires."

In doing these works, however, we must not think that a man is justified before God by them, for faith, which alone is righteousness before God, cannot endure that erroneous opinion. We must, however, realize that these works reduce the body to subjection and purify it of its evil lusts, and our whole purpose is to be directed only toward the driving out of lusts. Since by faith the soul is cleansed and made to love God, it desires that all things, and especially its own body, shall be purified so that all things may join with it in loving and praising God. Hence a man cannot be idle, for the need of his body drives him and he is compelled to do many good works to reduce it to subjection. Nevertheless the works themselves do not justify him before God, but he does the works out of spontaneous love in obedience to God and considers nothing except the approval of God, whom he would most scrupulously obey in all things.

In this way everyone will easily be able to learn for himself the limit and discretion, as they say, of his bodily castigations, for he will fast, watch, and labor as much as he finds sufficient to repress the lasciviousness and lust of his body. But those who presume to be justified by works do not regard the mortifying of the lusts, but only the works themselves, and think that if only they have done as many and as great works as are possible, they have done well and have become righteous. At times they even addle their brains and destroy, or at least render useless, their natural strength with their works. This is the height of folly and utter ignorance of Christian life and faith, that a man should seek to be justified and saved by works and without faith.

In order to make that which we have said more easily understood, we shall explain by analogies. We should think of the works of a Christian who is justified and saved by faith because of the pure and free mercy of God, just as we would think of the works which Adam and Eve did in Paradise, and all their children would have done if they had not sinned. We read in Gen. 2[:15] that "The Lord God took the man and put him in the garden of Eden to till it and keep it." Now Adam was created righteous and upright and without sin by God so that he had no need of being justified and made upright through his tilling and keeping the garden; but, that he might not be idle, the Lord gave him a task to do, to cultivate and protect the garden. This task would truly have been the freest of works, done only to please God and not to obtain righteousness, which Adam already had in full measure and which would have been the birthright of us all.

The works of a believer are like this. Through his faith he has been restored to Paradise and created anew, has no need of works that he may become or be righteous; but that he may not be idle and may provide for and keep his body, he must do such works freely only to please God. Since, however, we are not wholly recreated, and our faith and love are not yet perfect, these are to be increased, not by external works, however, but of themselves.

A second example: A bishop, when he consecrates a church, confirms children, or performs some other duty belonging to his office, is not made a bishop by these works. Indeed, if he had not first been made a bishop, none of these works would be valid. They would be foolish, childish, and farcical. So the Christian who is consecrated by his faith does good works, but the works do not make him holier or more Christian, for that is the work of faith alone. And if a man were not first a believer and a Christian, all his works would amount to nothing and would be truly wicked and damnable sins.

The following statements are therefore true: "Good works do not make a good man, but a good man does good works; evil works do not make a wicked man, but a wicked man does evil works." Consequently it is always necessary that the substance or person himself be good before there can be any good works, and that good works follow and proceed from the good person, as Christ also says, "A good tree cannot bear evil fruit, nor can a bad tree bear good fruit" [Matt. 7:18]. It is clear that the fruits do not bear the tree and that the tree does not grow on the fruits, also that, on the contrary, the trees bear the fruits and the fruits grow on the trees. As it is necessary, therefore, that the trees exist before their fruits and the fruits do not make trees either good or bad, but rather as the trees are, so are the fruits they bear; so a man must first be good or wicked before he does a good or wicked work, and his works do not make him good or wicked, but he himself makes his works either good or wicked.

Illustrations of the same truth can be seen in all trades. A good or a bad house does not make a good or a bad builder; but a good or a bad builder makes a good or a bad house. And in general, the work never makes the workman like itself, but the workman makes the work like himself. So it is with the works of man. As the man is, whether believer or unbeliever, so also is his work— good if it was done in faith, wicked if it was done in unbelief. But the converse is not true, that the work makes the man either a believer or an unbeliever. As works do not make a man a believer, so also they do not make him righteous. But as faith makes a man a believer and righteous, so faith does good works. Since, then, works justify no one, and a man must be righteous before he does a good work, it is very evident that it is faith alone which, because of the pure mercy of God through Christ and in his Word, worthily and sufficiently justifies and saves the person. A Christian has no need of any work or law in order to be saved since through faith he is free from every law and does everything out of pure liberty and freely. He seeks neither benefit nor salvation since he already abounds in all things and is saved through the grace of God because in his faith he now seeks only to please God.

Furthermore, no good work helps justify or save an unbeliever. On the other hand, no evil work makes him wicked or damns him; but the unbelief which makes the person and the tree evil does the evil and damnable works. Hence when a man is good or evil, this is effected not by the works, but by faith or unbelief, as the Wise Man says, "This is the beginning of sin, that a man falls away from God" [Cf. Sirach 10:14–15], which happens when he does not believe. And Paul says in Heb. 11[:6], "For whoever would draw near to God must believe. . . ." And Christ says the same: "Either make the tree good, and its fruit good; or make the tree bad, and its fruit bad" [Matt. 12:33], as if he would say, "Let him who wishes to have good fruit begin by planting a good tree." So let him who wishes to do good works begin not with the doing of works, but with believing, which makes the person good, for nothing makes a man good except faith, or evil except unbelief.

It is indeed true that in the sight of men a man is made good or evil by his works; but this being made good or evil only means that the man who is good or evil is pointed out and known as such, as Christ says in Matt. 7[:20], "Thus you will know them by their fruits." All this remains on the surface, however, and very many have been deceived by this outward appearance and have presumed to write and teach concerning good works by which we may be justified without even mentioning faith. They go their way, always being deceived and deceiving [II Tim. 3:13], progressing, indeed, but into a worse state, blind leaders of the blind, wearying themselves with many works and still never attaining to true righteousness [Matt. 15:14]. Of such people Paul says in II Tim. 3 [5, 7], "Holding the form of religion but denying the power of it . . . who will listen to anybody and can never arrive at a knowledge of the truth."

Whoever, therefore, does not wish to go astray with those blind men must look beyond works, and beyond laws and doctrines about works. Turning his eyes from works, he must look upon the person and ask how he is justified. For the person is justified and saved, not by works or laws, but by the Word of God, that is, by the promise of his grace, and by faith, that the glory may remain God's, who saved us not by works of righteousness which we have done [Titus 3:5], but by virtue of his mercy by the word of his grace when we believed [I Cor. 1:21].

From this it is easy to know how far good works are to be rejected or not, and by what standard all the teachings of men concerning works are to be interpreted. If works are sought after as a means to righteousness, are burdened with this perverse leviathan,[16] and are done under the false impression that through them one is justified, they are made necessary and freedom and faith are destroyed; and this addition to them makes them no longer good but truly damnable works. They are not free, and they blaspheme the grace of God since to justify and to save by faith belongs to the grace of God alone. What the works have no power to do they nevertheless—by a godless presumption through this folly of ours—pretend to do and thus violently force themselves into the office and glory of grace. We do not, therefore, reject good works;

on the contrary, we cherish and teach them as much as possible. We do not condemn them for their own sake but on account of this godless addition to them and the perverse idea that righteousness is to be sought through them; for that makes them appear good outwardly, when in truth they are not good. They deceive men and lead them to deceive one another like ravening wolves in sheep's clothing [Matt. 7:15].

But this leviathan, or perverse notion concerning works, is unconquerable where sincere faith is wanting. Those work-saints cannot get rid of it unless faith, its destroyer, comes and rules in their hearts. Nature of itself cannot drive it out or even recognize it, but rather regards it as a mark of the most holy will. If the influence of custom is added and confirms this perverseness of nature, as wicked teachers have caused it to do, it becomes an incurable evil and leads astray and destroys countless men beyond all hope of restoration. Therefore, although it is good to preach and write about penitence, confession, and satisfaction, our teaching is unquestionably deceitful and diabolical if we stop with that and do not go on to teach about faith.

Christ, like his forerunner John, not only said, "Repent" [Matt. 3:2; 4:17], but added the word of faith, saying, "The kingdom of heaven is at hand." We are not to preach only one of these words of God, but both; we are to bring forth out of our treasure things new and old, the voice of the law as well as the word of grace [Matt. 13:52]. We must bring forth the voice of the law that men may be made to fear and come to a knowledge of their sins and so be converted to repentance and a better life. But we must not stop with that, for that would only amount to wounding and not binding up, smiting and not healing, killing and not making alive, leading down into hell and not bringing back again, humbling and not exalting. Therefore we must also preach the word of grace and the promise of forgiveness by which faith is taught and aroused. Without this word of grace the works of the law, contrition, penitence, and all the rest are clone and taught in vain.

Preachers of repentance and grace remain even to our day, but they do not explain God's law and promise that a man might learn from them the source of repentance and grace. Repentance proceeds from the law of God, but faith or grace from the promise of God, as Rom. 10[:17] says: "So faith comes from what is heard, and what is heard comes by the preaching of Christ." Accordingly man is consoled and exalted by faith in the divine promise after he has been humbled and led to a knowledge of himself by the threats and the fear of the divine law. So we read in Psalm 30[:5]: "Weeping may tarry for the night, but joy comes with the morning."

Let this suffice concerning works in general and at the same time concerning the works which a Christian does for himself. Lastly, we shall also speak of the things which he does toward his neighbor. A man does not live for himself alone in tiffs mortal body to work for it alone, but he lives also for all men on earth; rather, he lives only for others and not for himself. To this end he brings his body into subjection that he may the more sincerely and freely serve others, as Paul says in Rom. 14[:7–8], "None of us lives to himself, and none of us dies to himself. If we live, we live to the Lord, and if we die, we die to the Lord." He cannot ever in this life be idle and without works toward his neighbors, for he will necessarily speak, deal with, and exchange views with men, as Christ also, being made in the likeness of men [Phil. 2:7], was found in form as a man and conversed with men, as Baruch 3[:38] says.

Man, however, needs none of these things for his righteousness and salvation. Therefore he should be guided in all his works by this thought and contemplate this one thing alone, that he may serve and benefit others in all that he does, considering nothing except the need and the advantage of his neighbor. Accordingly the Apostle commands us to work with our hands so that we may give to the needy, although he might have said that we should work to support ourselves. He says, however, "that he may be able to give to those in need" [Eph. 4:28]. This is what makes caring for the body a

Christian work, that through its health and comfort we may
be able to work, to acquire, and lay by funds with which to
aid those who are in need, that in this way the strong member
may serve the weaker, and we may be sons of God, each eating
for and working for the other, bearing one another's burdens
and so fulfilling the law of Christ [Gal. 6:2]. This is a truly
Christian life. Here faith is truly active through love [Gal.
5:6], that is, it finds expression in works of the freest service,
cheerfully and lovingly done, with which a man willingly
serves another without hope of reward; and for himself he is
satisfied with the fullness and wealth of his faith.

Accordingly Paul, after teaching the Philippians how rich
they were made through faith in Christ, in which they obtained
all things, thereafter teaches them, saying, "So if there is any
encouragement in Christ, any incentive of love, any participation in the Spirit, any affection and sympathy, complete my
joy by being of the same mind, having the same love, being
in full accord and of one mind. Do nothing from selfishness
or conceit, but in humility count others better than yourselves.
Let each of you look not only to his own interests, but also
to the interests of others" [Phil. 2:1–4]. Here we see clearly
that the Apostle has prescribed this rule for the life of Christians,
namely, that we should devote all our works to the welfare of
others, since each has such abundant riches in his faith that
all his other works and his whole life are a surplus with which
he can by voluntary benevolence serve and do good to his
neighbor.

As an example of such life the Apostle cites Christ, saying,
"Have this mind among yourselves, which you have in Christ
Jesus, who, though he was in the form of God, did not count
equality with God a thing to be grasped, but emptied himself,
taking the form of a servant, being born in the likeness of
men. And being found in human form he humbled himself
and became obedient unto death" [Phil. 2:5–8]. This salutary
word of the Apostle has been obscured for us by those who
have not at all understood his words, "form of God," "form

of a servant," "human form," "likeness of men," and have applied them to the divine and the human nature. Paul means this: Although Christ was filled with the form of God and rich in all good things, so that he needed no work and no suffering to make him righteous and saved (for he had all this eternally), yet he was not puffed up by them and did not exalt himself above us and assume power over us, although he could rightly have done so; but, on the contrary, he so lived, labored, worked, suffered, and died that he might be like other men and in fashion and in actions be nothing else than a man, just as if he had need of all these things and had nothing of the form of God. But he did all this for our sake, that he might serve us and that all things which he accomplished in this form of a servant might become ours.

So a Christian, like Christ his head, is filled and made rich by faith and should be content with this form of God which he has obtained by faith; only, as I have said, he should increase this faith until it is made perfect. For this faith is his life, his righteousness, and his salvation: it saves him and makes him acceptable, and bestows upon him all things that are Christ's, as has been said above, and as Paul asserts in Gal. 2[:20] when he says, "And the life I now live in the flesh I live by faith in the Son of God." Although the Christian is thus free from all works, he ought in this liberty to empty himself, take upon himself the form of a servant, be made in the likeness of men, be found in human form, and to serve, help, and in every way deal with his neighbor as he sees that God through Christ has dealt and still deals with him. This he should do freely, having regard for nothing but divine approval.

He ought to think: "Although I am an unworthy and condemned man, my God has given me in Christ all the riches of righteousness and salvation without any merit on my part, out of pure, free mercy, so that from now on I need nothing except faith which believes that this is true. Why should I not therefore freely, joyfully, with all my heart, and with an eager will do all things which I know are pleasing and acceptable to such a Father who has overwhelmed me with his inestimable riches? I will therefore give myself as a Christ to my neighbor, just as Christ offered himself to me; I will do nothing in this life except what I see is necessary, profitable, and salutary to my neighbor, since through faith I have an abundance of all good things in Christ."

Behold, from faith thus flow forth love and joy in the Lord, and from love a joyful, willing, and free mind that serves one's neighbor willingly and takes no account of gratitude or ingratitude, of praise or blame, of gain or loss. For a man does not serve that he may put men under obligations. He does not distinguish between friends and enemies or anticipate their thankfulness or unthankfulness, but he most freely and most willingly spends himself and all that he has, whether he wastes all on the thankless or whether he gains a reward. As his Father does, distributing all things to all men richly and freely, making "his sun rise on the evil and on the good" [Matt. 5:45], so also the son does all things and suffers all things with that freely bestowing joy which is his delight when through Christ he sees it in God, the dispenser of such great benefits.

Therefore, if we recognize the great and precious things which are given us, as Paul says [Rom. 5:5], our hearts will be filled by the Holy Spirit with the love which makes us free, joyful, almighty workers and conquerors over all tribulations, servants of our neighbors, and yet lords of all. For those who do not recognize the gifts bestowed upon them through Christ, however, Christ has been born in vain; they go their way with their works and shall never come to taste or feel those things. Just as our neighbor is in need and lacks that in which we abound, so we were in need before God and lacked his mercy. Hence, as our heavenly Father has in Christ freely come to our aid, we also ought freely to help our neighbor through our body and its works, and each one should become as it were a Christ to the other that we may be Christs to one another and Christ may be the same in all, that is, that we may be truly Christians.

Who then can comprehend the riches and the glory of the Christian life? It can do all things and has all things and lacks nothing. It is lord over sin, death, and hell, and yet at the same time it serves, ministers to, and benefits all men. But alas in our day this life is unknown throughout the world; it is neither preached about nor sought after; we are altogether ignorant of our own name and do not know why we are Christians or bear the name of Christians. Surely we are named after Christ, not because he is absent from us, but because he dwells in us, that is, because we believe in him and are Christs one to another and do to our neighbors as Christ does to us. But in our day we are taught by the doctrine of men to seek nothing but merits, rewards, and the things that are ours; of Christ we have made only a taskmaster far harsher than Moses.

We have a pre-eminent example of such a faith in the blessed Virgin. As is written in Luke 2[:22], she was purified according to the law of Moses according to the custom of all women, although she was not bound by that law and did not need to be purified. Out of free and willing love, however, she submitted to the law like other women that she might not offend or despise them. She was not justified by this work, but being righteous she did it freely and willingly. So also our works should be done, not that we may be justified by them, since, being justified beforehand by faith, we ought to do all things freely and joyfully for the sake of others.

St. Paul also circumcised his disciple Timothy, not because circumcision was necessary for his righteousness, but that he might not offend or despise the Jews who were weak in the faith and could not yet grasp the liberty of faith. But, on the other hand, when they despised the liberty of faith and insisted that circumcision was necessary for righteousness, he resisted them and did not allow Titus to be circumcised (Gal. 2[:3]). Just as he was unwilling to offend or despise any man's weak faith and yielded to their will for a time, so he was also unwilling that the liberty of faith should be offended against or despised by stubborn, work-righteous men. He chose a middle way, sparing the weak for a time, but always withstanding the stubborn, that he might convert all to the liberty of faith. What we do should be done with the same zeal to sustain the weak in faith, as in Rom. 14[:1]; but we should firmly resist the stubborn teachers of works. Of this we shall say more later.

Christ also, in Matt. 17[:24–27], when the tax money was demanded of his disciples, discussed with St. Peter whether the sons of the king were not free from the payment of tribute, and Peter affirmed that they were. Nonetheless, Christ commanded Peter to go to the sea and said, "Not to give offense to them, go to the sea and cast a hook, and take the first fish that comes up, and when you open its mouth you will find a shekel; take that and give it to them for me and for yourself." This incident fits our subject beautifully for Christ here calls himself and those who are his children sons of the king, who need nothing; and yet he freely submits and pays the tribute. Just as necessary and helpful as this work was to Christ's righteousness or salvation, just so much do all other works of his or his followers avail for righteousness, since they all follow after righteousness and are free and are done only to serve others and to give them an example of good works.

Of the same nature are the precepts which Paul gives in Rom. 13[:1–7], namely, that Christians should be subject to the governing authorities and be ready to do every good work, not that they shall in this way be justified, since they already are righteous through faith, but that in the liberty of the Spirit they shall by so doing serve others and the authorities themselves and obey their will freely and out of love. The works of all colleges,[17] monasteries, and priests should be of this nature. Each one should do the works of his profession and station, not that by them he may strive after righteousness, but that through them he may keep his body under control, be an example to others who also need to keep their bodies under control, and finally that by such works he may submit his will to that of others in the freedom of love. But very great care must always be exercised so that no man in a false confidence imagines that by such works he will be justified or acquire merit or be saved; for this is the work of faith alone, as I have repeatedly said.

Anyone knowing this could easily and without danger find his way through those numberless mandates and precepts of pope, bishops, monasteries, churches, princes, and magistrates upon which some ignorant pastors insist as if they were necessary to righteousness and salvation, calling them "precepts of the church," although they are nothing of the kind. For a Christian, as a free man, will say, "I will fast, pray, do this and that as men command, not because it is necessary to my righteousness or salvation; but that I may show due respect to the pope, the bishop, the community, a magistrate, or my neighbor, and give them an example. I will do and suffer all things, just as Christ did and suffered far more for me, although he needed nothing of it all for himself, and was made under the law for my sake, although he was not under the law." Although tyrants do violence or injustice in making their demands, yet it will do no harm as long as they demand nothing contrary to God.

From what has been said, everyone can pass a safe judgment on all works and laws and make a trustworthy distinction between them and know who are the blind and ignorant pastors and who are the good and true. Any work that is not done solely for the purpose of keeping the body under control or of serving one's neighbor, as long as he asks nothing contrary to God, is not good or Christian. For this reason I greatly fear that few or no colleges, monasteries, altars, and offices of the church are really Christian in our day—nor the special fasts and prayers on certain saints' days. I fear, I say, that in all these we seek only our profit, thinking that through them our sins are purged away and that we find salvation in them. In this way Christian liberty perishes altogether. This is a consequence of our ignorance of Christian faith and liberty.

This ignorance and suppression of liberty very many blind pastors take pains to encourage. They stir up and urge on their people in these practices by praising such works, puffing them up with their indulgences, and never teaching faith. If, however, you wish to pray, fast, or establish a foundation in the church, I advise you to be careful not to do it in order to obtain some benefit, whether temporal or eternal, for you would do injury to your faith which alone offers you all things. Your one care should be that faith may grow, whether it is trained by works or sufferings. Make your gifts freely and for no consideration, so that others may profit by them and fare well because of you and your goodness. In this way you shall be truly good and Christian. Of what benefit to you are the good works which you do not need for keeping your body under control? Your faith is sufficient for you, through which God has given you all things.

See, according to this rule the good things we have from God should flow from one to the other and be common to all, so that everyone should "put on" his neighbor and so conduct himself toward him as if he himself were in the other's place. From Christ the good things have flowed and are flowing into us. He has so "put on" us and acted for us as if he had been what we are. From us they flow on to those who have need of them so that I should lay before God my faith and my righteousness that they may cover and intercede for the sins of my neighbor which I take upon myself and so labor and serve in them as if they were my very own. That is what Christ did for us. This is true love and the genuine rule of a Christian life. Love is true and genuine where there is true and genuine faith. Hence the Apostle says of love in I Cor. 13[:5] that "it does not seek its own."

We conclude, therefore, that a Christian lives not in himself, but in Christ and in his neighbor. Otherwise he is not a Christian. He lives in Christ through faith, in his neighbor through love. By faith he is caught up beyond himself into God. By love he descends beneath himself into his neighbor. Yet he

always remains in God and in his love, as Christ says in John
1[:51], "Truly, truly, I say to you, you will see heaven opened,
and the angels of God ascending and descending upon the
Son of man."

Enough now of freedom. As you see, it is a spiritual and
true freedom and makes our hearts free from all sins, laws
and commands, as Paul says, I Tim. 1[:9], "The law is not
laid down for the just." It is more excellent than all other
liberty, which is external, as heaven is more excellent than
earth. May Christ give us this liberty both to understand and
to preserve. Amen.

Finally, something must be added for the sake of those for
whom nothing can be said so well that they will not spoil it
by misunderstanding it. It is questionable whether they will
understand even what will be said here. There are very many
who, when they hear of this freedom of faith, immediately
turn it into an occasion for the flesh and think that now all
things are allowed them. They want to show that they are free
men and Christians only by despising and finding fault with
ceremonies, traditions, and human laws; as if they were Christians because on stated days they do not fast or eat meat when
others fast, or because they do not use the accustomed prayers,
and with upturned nose scoff at the precepts of men, although
they utterly disregard all else that pertains to the Christian
religion. The extreme opposite of these are those who rely for
their salvation solely on their reverent observance of ceremonies, as if they would be saved because on certain days they
fast or abstain from meats, or pray certain prayers; these make
a boast of the precepts of the church and of the fathers, and
do not care a fig for the things which are of the essence of our
faith. Plainly, both are in error because they neglect the weight-
ier things which are necessary to salvation, and quarrel so
noisily about trifling and unnecessary matters.

How much better is the teaching of the Apostle Paul who
bids us take a middle course and condemns both sides when
he says, "Let not him who eats despise him who abstains, and

let not him who abstains pass judgment on him who eats"
[Rom. 14:3]. Here you see that they who neglect and disparage
ceremonies, not out of piety, but out of mere contempt, are
reproved, since the Apostle teaches us not to despise them.
Such men are puffed up by knowledge. On the other hand,
he teaches those who insist on the ceremonies not to judge
the others, for neither party acts toward the other according
to the love that edifies. Wherefore we ought to listen to Scripture which teaches that we should not go aside to the right
or to the left [Deut. 28:14] but follow the statutes of the Lord
which are right, "rejoicing the heart" [Ps. 19:8]. As a man is
not righteous because he keeps and clings to the works and
forms of the ceremonies, so also will a man not be counted
righteous merely because he neglects and despises them.

Our faith in Christ does not free us from works but from
false opinions concerning works, that is, from the foolish
presumption that justification is acquired by works. Faith
redeems, corrects, and preserves our consciences so that we
know that righteousness does not consist in works, although
works neither can nor ought to be wanting; just as we cannot
be without food and drink and all the works of this mortal
body, yet our righteousness is not in them, but in faith; and
yet those works of the body are not to be despised or neglected
on that account. In this world we are bound by the needs of
our bodily life, but we are not righteous because of them.
"My kingship is not of this world" [John 18:36], says Christ.
He does not, however, say, "My kingship is not here, that is,
in this world." And Paul says, "Though we live in the world
we are not carrying on a worldly war" [II Cor. 10:3], and in
Gal. 2[:20], "The life I now live in the flesh I live by faith in
the Son of God." Thus what we do, live, and are in works and
ceremonies, we do because of the necessities of this life and
of the effort to rule our body. Nevertheless we are righteous,
not in these, but in the faith of the Son of God.

Hence the Christian must take a middle course and face
those two classes of men. He will meet first the unyielding,

stubborn ceremonialists who like deaf adders are not willing to hear the truth of liberty [Ps. 58:4] but, having no faith, boast of, prescribe, and insist upon their ceremonies as means of justification. Such were the Jews of old, who were unwilling to learn how to do good. These he must resist, do the very opposite, and offend them boldly lest by their impious views they drag many with them into error. In the presence of such men it is good to eat meat, break the fasts, and for the sake of the liberty of faith do other things which they regard as the greatest of sins. Of them we must say, "Let them alone; they are blind guides." According to this principle Paul would not circumcise Titus when the Jews insisted that he should [Gal. 2:3], and Christ excused the apostles when they plucked ears of grain on the sabbath [Matt. 12:1–8]. There are many similar instances. The other class of men whom a Christian will meet are the simple-minded, ignorant men, weak in the faith, as the Apostle calls them, who cannot yet grasp the liberty of faith, even if they were willing to do so [Rom. 14:1]. These he must take care not to offend. He must yield to their weakness until they are more fully instructed. Since they do and think as they do, not because they are stubbornly wicked, but only because their faith is weak, the fasts and other things which they consider necessary must be observed to avoid giving them offense. This is the command of love which would harm no one but would serve all men. It is not by their fault that they are weak, but by that of their pastors who have taken them captive with the snares of their traditions and have wickedly used these traditions as rods with which to beat them. They should have been delivered from these pastors by the teachings of faith and freedom. So the Apostle teaches us in Romans 14: "If food is a cause of my brother's falling, I will never eat meat" [Cf. Rom. 14:21 and I Cor. 8:13]; and again, "I know and am persuaded in the Lord Jesus that nothing is unclean in itself; but it is unclean for any one who thinks it unclean" [Rom. 14:14].

For this reason, although we should boldly resist those teachers of traditions and sharply censure the laws of the popes by means of which they plunder the people of God, yet we must spare the timid multitude whom those impious tyrants hold captive by means of these laws until they are set free. Therefore fight strenuously against the wolves, but for the sheep and not also against the sheep. This you will do if you inveigh against the laws and the lawgivers and at the same time observe the laws with the weak so that they will not be offended, until they also recognize tyranny and understand their freedom. If you wish to use your freedom, do so in secret, as Paul says, Rom. 14[:22], "The faith that you have, keep between yourself and God"; but take care not to use your freedom in the sight of the weak. On the other hand, use your freedom constantly and consistently in the sight of and despite the tyrants and the stubborn so that they also may learn that they are impious, that their laws are of no avail for righteousness, and that they had no right to set them up.

Since we cannot live our lives without ceremonies and works, and the perverse and untrained youth need to be restrained and saved from harm by such bonds; and since each one should keep his body under control by means of such works, there is need that the minister of Christ be farseeing and faithful. He ought so to govern and teach Christians in all these matters that their conscience and faith will not be offended and that there will not spring up in them a suspicion and a root of bitterness and many will thereby be defiled, as Paul admonishes the Hebrews [Heb. 12:15]; that is, that they may not lose faith and become defiled by the false estimate of the value of works and think that they must be justified by works. Unless faith is at the same time constantly taught, this happens easily and defiles a great many, as has been done until now through the pestilent, impious, soul-destroying traditions of our popes and the opinions of our theologians. By these snares numberless souls have been dragged down to hell, so that you might see in this the work of Antichrist.

In brief, as wealth is the test of poverty, business the test of faithfulness, honors the test of humility, feasts the test of temperance, pleasures the test of chastity, so ceremonies are the test of the righteousness of faith. "Can a man," asks Solomon, "carry fire in his bosom and his clothes and not be burned?" [Prov. 6:27]. Yet as a man must live in the midst of wealth, business, honors, pleasures, and feasts, so also must he live in the midst of ceremonies, that is, in the midst of dangers. Indeed, as infant boys need beyond all else to be cherished in the bosoms and by the hands of maidens to keep them from perishing, yet when they are grown up their salvation is endangered if they associate with maidens, so the inexperienced and perverse youth need to be restrained and trained by the iron bars of ceremonies lest their unchecked ardor rush headlong into vice after vice. On the other hand, it would be death for them always to be held in bondage to ceremonies, thinking that these justify them. They are rather to be taught that they have been so imprisoned in ceremonies, not that they should be made righteous or gain great merit by them, but that they might thus be kept from doing evil and might more easily be instructed to the righteousness of faith. Such instruction they would not endure if the impulsiveness of their youth were not restrained.

Hence ceremonies are to be given the same place in the life of a Christian as models and plans have among builders and artisans. They are prepared, not as a permanent structure, but because without them nothing could be built or made. When the structure is complete the models and plans are laid aside. You see, they are not despised, rather they are greatly sought after; but what we despise is the false estimate of them since no one holds them to be the real and permanent structure.

If any man were so flagrantly foolish as to care for nothing all his life long except the most costly, careful, and persistent preparation of plans and models and never to think of the structure itself, and were satisfied with his work in producing such plans and mere aids to work, and boasted of it, would

not all men pity his insanity and think that something great
might have been built with what he has wasted? Thus we do
not despise ceremonies and works, but we set great store by
them; but we despise the false estimate placed upon works in
order that no one may think that they are true righteousness,
as those hypocrites believe who spend and lose their whole
lives in zeal for works and never reach that goal for the sake
of which the works are to be done, who, as the Apostle says,
"will listen to anybody and can never arrive at a knowledge
of the truth" [II Tim. 3:7]. They seem to wish to build, they
make their preparations, and yet they never build. Thus they
remain caught in the form of religion and do not attain unto
its power [II Tim. 3:5]. Meanwhile they are pleased with their
efforts and even dare to judge all others whom they do not
see shining with a like show of works. Yet with the gifts of
God which they have spent and abused in vain they might, if
they had been filled with faith, have accomplished great things
to their own salvation and that of others.

Since human nature and natural reason, as it is called, are
by nature superstitious and ready to imagine, when laws
and works are prescribed, that righteousness must be obtained
through laws and works; and further, since they are trained
and confirmed in this opinion by the practice of all earthly
lawgivers, it is impossible that they should of themselves es-
cape from the slavery of works and come to a knowledge of
the freedom of faith. Therefore there is need of the prayer
that the Lord may give us and make us *theodidacti*, that is,
those taught by God [John 6:45], and himself, as he has
promised, write his law in our hearts; otherwise there is no
hope for us. If he himself does not teach our hearts this wisdom hidden in mystery [I Cor. 2:7], nature can only condemn
it and judge it to be heretical because nature is offended by
it and regards it as foolishness. So we see that it happened in
the old days in the case of the apostles and prophets, and so
godless and blind popes and their flatterers do to me and to
those who are like me. May God at last be merciful to them

and to us and cause his face to shine upon us that we may
know his way upon earth [Ps. 67:1–2], his salvation among
all nations, God, who is blessed forever [II Cor. 11:31]. Amen.

## Notes

1. The given name of Mühlphordt was Hermann, not Hieronymus, as Luther has it.

2. In place of the German version of the treatise which Luther
sent to Mühlphordt, the Latin version dedicated to the pope is
used as the basis of the English translation in this volume.

3. Sylvester Mazzolini (1456–1523), usually called Prierias after
Prierio, the city of his birth, had published three books against
Luther. In these he had exaggerated the authority of the papacy.

4. An attempt to poison Leo X had been made in the summer
of 1517.

5. Bernard of Clairvaux wrote a devotional book, *On
Consideration*, to Pope Eugenius III (1145–53), in which he
discussed the duties of the pope and the dangers connected with
his office. Migne 182, 727–808.

6. [[See page 336 of original . . .—Eds.]].

7. Thraso, in the original, is the name of a braggart soldier in
Terence's *Eunuch*.

8. Cardinal Cajetan, [[See page 264 of original . . .—Eds.]].

9. Karl von Miltitz had induced Luther to be silent with respect
to the indulgence controversy, provided his opponents did likewise.
Cf. above, [[See page 310 of original . . .—Eds.]] and [[See page
329 of original . . .—Eds.]].

10. At Altenburg on January 5 or 6, 1519.

11. *Servus servorum* was the usual title of the pope.

12. [[See page 887 of original . . .—Eds.]].

13. *The Freedom of a Christian.*

14. Luther was fond of Aesop's Fables, of which this is one.

15. [[See page 352 of original . . .—Eds.]].

16. Probably a reminiscence of Leviathan, the twisting serpent,
in Isa. 27:1.

17. The word "college" here denotes a corporation of clergy
supported by a foundation and performing certain religious
services.

# III

Grace and Gratitude:
Appropriating Luther's
Spirituality Today

Martin Luther grew up in the fifteenth century and flourished in the sixteenth. His theology cannot be translated into the twenty-first century with a consistent one-to-one correspondence. Denominational Lutherans may or may not recognize the accents of their churches in the retrievals that follow. But these classic texts still evoke resonance in the spiritualities of people who live in a secular, religiously pluralistic, and pragmatic culture and in societies that reflect urban values. These circumstances describe the context and the challenge that this commentary addresses.

Religious sociologists know that Luther lives in the lives of many who actively and in full measure participate in public life today. But demonstrating how Luther's ideas are being formally integrated into current patterns of life requires some creative imagining. The interpretive strategy used here moves in two directions at once, in a simultaneous back and forth. It looks back at Luther from the present and appropriates what seems fitting for Christian life today,[1] and it also projects Luther's ideas and language forward to question what is happening around us.

## Dialectical Imagination and Negative Experiences of Contrast

The question of why the phenomenon of Martin Luther occurred is answered from many perspectives with different theories. It makes sense religiously, in terms of faith and belief, to think of Luther being impelled by the logic of scandal. He looked out on the contemporary theology, spirituality, and devotional practices of the church, which included the practice of selling indulgences, and was shocked. Matthew's gospel has Jesus promising Peter about the church that "the gates of the netherworld shall not prevail against it" (Matt 16:18). Luther had to think that the church in Rome was not the true church because it seemed to have succumbed to the forces of the devil. Luther had what present-day theology calls a negative experience of contrast.[2]

A negative experience of contrast points in broad strokes to a structure of moral sensibility. But it applies neatly to spiritual experience with terms that describe particular instances of being scandalized. It consists of three dimensions of consciousness that simultaneously interact with each other. One can be noted as simply a recognition that something is wrong: in my life, in a personal relationship, or in a social situation. These negative experiences can range from the trivial to the profound, as, for example, in what leads to the dissolution of a marriage. It may be a massive social consciousness like the realization of the moral depravity of slavery that sustained the American Civil War. But such a negative reaction can only happen or exist on the basis of a sensibility that things could be different, a positive conviction that there is a better way, even if one does not know exactly what that would be. One cannot really appreciate that something should not be without a sense of the good that offers some alternative. One more theme contributes to a full experience of this negative contrast: a desire or impulse to change it, to right the wrong, to the best of one's ability.

On a descriptive level one can locate such an experience as part of the fundamental equipment of being human. It may be rooted in life itself as an instinct for doing what is necessary for the survival of the self, group, or species. In human beings what seems to be a negative principle really accounts for a positive moral sensibility. The negative finds its roots in a constructive sense of what ought, should, and even could be the case if one committed oneself to overcoming the impasse. Looked on in this light, the opinion that Luther's conception of faith renders a person passive or unengaged simply vanishes. Faith as trust in the face of the negativity of sin stimulates the agent precisely toward addressing and overcoming the problem.

Negative contrast experiences correlate with the dialectical dimension of the imagination. On the social level, the dialectical imagination belongs to the prophet, village watchman, and whistleblower, who has seen the problem and been energized to negate the negation and right the wrong. When problems affected theological understanding causing a lifeless separation between doctrine and experience, Luther turned to scripture for revitalization. If the problem concerned unethical practices among clerics and the institutions of the church, this called for reform. If the devotional practices of the church objectified spirituality, rendering it mechanical rather than existentially meaningful, Luther called for change and spiritual animation of corporate parish life. Without minimizing the particular genius of Luther, the time had become ripe for reform.

## Faith and Works

The ongoing discussion related to Luther's distinction between faith and works sometimes gets translated into alternatives between emphasizing proclamation and emphasizing social justice. This misreads the holistic theology of Luther as competing dimensions that should be held together. Luther's spirituality recognizes the integral unity of the inner and outer person in a theological anthropology; justification and the outflowing manifestations of God's grace in holy human activity make up a single response. Grace does not remove the need for action but overflows into it. For Luther the outer works reflect the inner person and the regenerative power that comes from total reliance on God's grace in Christ. The distinction emphasizes the spiritual character of faith even when it is directed toward social reform.

In a close analysis of a Christian's spirituality, the distinction between faith and works and everything that Luther packed into this distinction make good sense. But it can degenerate into a rather fine if not archaic theological discussion. How can churches that for the most part agree on the priority of grace divide over such a theological debate? This current reflection does not minimize the scandalous character of the practice of selling indulgences back then, which in its crass form was corrected. But that leaves open the question of whether this distinction, so important for Luther, can be brought forward into our time with constructive purpose. A presupposition and two reflections yield a positive response to this question.

First: a supposition. Theology in the twentieth century caught up with an emergent planetary consciousness. Human beings have become conscious of the unity of the human race in a vivid new way through evolutionary life sciences and the media of relatively instant global communication. In all our differences, we are one species trying to get along with each other, other species, and the world itself. But this newly discovered empirical interconnectedness, especially in the light of a Christian consciousness of one Creator present to all reality, almost demands a supposition that God's favor, love, and grace accompanies God's creating presence to all. The love of God for God's creation which is "good" seems like a cornerstone to all Christian beliefs. The universal offer of

God's grace represents more than a theological opinion; only narrow traditionalist churches today imagine God for themselves to the exclusion of others. While that makes no sense today, it was a nonreflective supposition of most theology in the sixteenth century. By contrast, on the supposition of God's grace at work in all people, how can Luther's duality of faith and works nourish spirituality in our time?

*The two-fold relationship of human existence.* A first constructive move consists of slightly revising Luther's distinction between an inner and an outer person. While this distinction is workable on some level of common sense, it appears problematic from the perspective of developmental psychology where inner and outer are bound together. It can promote an a priori dualism or antagonistic relationship between soul and body, the spiritual and the material. This remains an issue in the history of Christian spirituality. But a better way of preserving what Luther intends here, speaking in terms that are both commonsensical and metaphysical, would be to speak of one human existence, or one human person, in a two-fold relationship. The distinction is drawn from inside the circle of Christian faith. It says that human existence itself, or the individual human person, simultaneously exists as being in relation to God and being in relation to the surrounding world.

This revision of Luther's construct preserves his intention of formulating a platform for making expansive inclusive statements about human existence before God. It also has the advantage of not appearing to divide the person into "parts"; the subject matter is never the outer or inner person; it is always the person. Various spheres in which the human person operates are differentiated, surely enough, but always with reference to the person. Since one person is constituted in these relationships, they are always simultaneously in play. One does not relate to the world outside of one's being in relation to God, and one cannot be the person one is before God without bringing along all one's relationships to the world. These worldly relationships define in part who a person is and thus contribute to each person's identity. This revision of Luther's distinction also allows the preservation of Luther's conception of two kingdoms. The human person must attend to his or her relationship to the world, referring to all the operations of daily life. All persons should also attend to the relationship by which they are constituted in being, to what ultimately determines one's being. But these two codetermining relationships, even when they occupy distinct periods of attention, cannot be separated from each other in defining who a person is.

*Dependence on God and self-reliance: breaking this alternative.* A second point applies this distinction of relationships to psychologically or reflectively conscious spirituality. Luther's reflections on how Christians relate to God within the two-fold relationship are extremely helpful at this point. One way to sort this out consists of comparing the ideas of dependence on God and self-reliance.

Luther showed that a separation of these two forms of consciousness spells spiritual disaster. Striving on one's own to merit God's favor is delusory. Clinging to God in a way that reneges on the responsibilities of everyday life contradicts the very intention of the God one adores. In more expansive terms, these are the theses that *The Freedom of a Christian* defends. The person who would be lord of all without being dependent on God is a fool; holding on to God without being servant of all is equally fraudulent and ruinous.

But we learn still more by turning to look at how faith and works are united. Their coinherence and reciprocal interaction contribute positively and constructively to a wholesome Christian spirituality in our time. This entails breaking the alternative between works and faith, or faith and works, and recognizing how they reinforce each other on a conscious level. This does not mean that grace and human freedom are two agencies working on the same plane. One has to stipulate that grace describes the a priori condition of human existence itself; and God cannot be considered an agent alongside human freedom. In Christian spirituality according to Luther, dependence on God's grace bestows psychological self-reliance; it makes each one *somebody*. God does not subtract from human agency, but bestows, supports, and strengthens it. And from an anthropological perspective, recognizing one's absolute dependence on God does not pit one against social responsibility but encourages and supports it. In fact, Christian faith says that the love of God for us commands it.

## A Positive Relation to the World

Luther inspires a positive spiritual relationship with the world that correlates with the relationship between faith and works. Luther differentiated between one's spiritual relationship with God and the large sphere of human involvement with the world. The term *world* codified both a domain of competition, greed, and sin as well as the neutral social order of family, work, and politics. He rejected the idea that living a good moral life according to the law of itself united one with God, but he promoted a spirituality of faith that overflowed in love and service of the neighbor. How does this latter positive formula inform Christian spirituality in a world that has been completely transformed by science and historical consciousness? This seemingly theoretical question actually haunts many Christians who do not know how to integrate a scientific worldview into their faith or the pragmatic secular activity that occupies so much of their lives into a relationship with God.

A response to this issue builds on the previous distinction of one single conscious being that exists in a two-fold relationship. This formula purely and simply overcomes a kind of split personality or radical distinctions of worlds or spheres of activity from each other. It is true that people budget their time between tasks, but each single person is equipped to enter into and carry forward many different relationships.

A second principle from the previous discussion also has an important bearing on fundamental attitudes toward the world, namely, the universality of the offer of God's saving grace. This principle makes sense to a Christian imagination that considers the doctrine of creation. Grace in this proposition is not limited to forgiveness of sin but affirms that God loves what God creates and cannot not love it. Far from minimizing the reality of sin or undermining the doctrine of forgiveness, it renders forgiveness coherent. Forgiveness from God in the Christian imagination springs from God's love. It is true that human beings can be overwhelmed by the gratuity of God's forgiveness. They also have to wonder about how human experiences of justice and mercy can be applied to the absolute mystery of God. The dualism between good and evil in Christian faith describes a moral world and does not set up evil as a rival to God. Love characterizes the very nature of God in the Christian faith tradition, even though people frequently encounter conditions that make this hard to believe. It seems entirely correct to think that God loves all sinners, despite their sins, with divine love.

These considerations support Luther's positive conception of how Christian faith situates a person in relation to the world. They show how his view responds to some basic questions, such as, for example, how one can encounter God within the world. Science describes the world as emergent and evolutionary as it breaks forth into life. It affirms that human existence is part of the material world. Christian faith appropriates that proposal in terms of God's ongoing or continual creation. Human existence has evolved as precisely that part of God's creation with a reflective consciousness that can be aware of and respond to God. Being in a conscious relation to God does not set one apart from the world; rather, God creates human beings in the world, out of the material of the world, to be in it as part of it. These words, of course, reflect the completely incomprehensible mystery that is God and God creating; but they also affirm that our being in the world is not aberrant or a misfortune, but our very being as God's creatures. Human existence does not stand over against the world but is that part of the world that can exist in a reflective conscious relation to its transcendent creator.

It helps to recall Luther's thinking at this precise point. Luther rejected a spirituality of complete reliance on our life in the world. He rejected a reduction of the inner person to the outer depiction of a person in either moral or scientific terms. Rather he affirmed a Christian's full engagement in the world in a way that did not suppress but built upon the fundamental relationship with God that constitutes and grounds one's very participation in the world. The human person is a conscious being constituted in being as dependent on God and fully a part of the world created to participate in the world.

One of the problems of Luther's theology and spirituality arises from a fixation on his reaction to some of the church practices of his time. But his negative experiences of contrast, which were themselves differentiated across personal, spiritual, and social spheres, spawned positive constructions that should command attention. To be related to God does not negate but promotes positive relationships to the world. Being related to a creating and loving God does not abstract one from the world but injects one into the world positively, constructively, as an active agent of God's love for the world. Once the presupposition of God's universal love and grace is in place, a liberation theology bears no Pelagian overtones in Luther's constructive vision. Eco-spirituality actually extends a spirituality of faith into the sphere of love of neighbor as Luther described it. This love of neighbor assumes responsibility for shared life into the future. A militant stance against racism or abuse of women in the world does not negate Christian faith's clinging to Christ's revelation of God but extends it out into the world. Reading Luther as standing against a world and science that threaten or negate spirituality grossly misinterprets what he proposes. As for fundamental attitudes toward the world, Luther's insight that faith in God makes one lord of the world with nothing to fear describes incisively what is needed in today's world. Faith's relation to God provides a distinctive kind of courage that is needed to promote God's will for the world today.

## Theocentrism and Christomorphism

Today's intellectual culture, the broad outlook of people educated in the humanities and sciences, presents a worldview that differs considerably from the one that prevailed in the sixteenth century. Copernicus was born ten years before Luther in 1473, and during the 1530s his heliocentric views were beginning to circulate in Europe. Luther outrightly rejected his ideas. Since then, by slow and steady progression, science has utterly transformed the human perception of the universe and the planet on which we live. A gradual transformation has also affected human perception of what it means for human beings to live in history. People have come to recognize the effect that social and cultural conditions have on perception and understanding. At one end of a spectrum, the deep diversity that affects global convictions about matters of basic importance lead many to become relativists. Others have been led to a more balanced and positive respect for other cultures, acceptance of difference, and appreciation of the value of pluralism. They recognize the unity of the species and many shared ideas and values. Historical consciousness teaches that in principle one should acknowledge that cultures and religions bear dimensions of truth of which other cultures are ignorant. On large theoretical and religious matters especially, an absolutist mentality has been attenuated; faith traditions have become more open to others and shown a willingness to enter a dialogue in order to learn. This hardly implies that group bias has disappeared or that every religious vision makes sense. But we no longer live in the sixteenth century.

*Grace-filled naturalism.* One way of adjusting theological understanding to a culture influenced by science and historical consciousness lies in setting up the context for the discussion; it has to have a universal reach and offer an accessible metaphysical insight. That can be found in the Christian doctrine of creation out of nothing. Everyone can ask why the universe exists at all. The doctrine of creation always exists within particular faith traditions, but it appeals to a universal anthropological experience of contingency and finitude that, like Luther's outer and inner personhood, has a metaphysical character. The doctrine of creation says that all of reality directly depends on God's creating causality. This is unimaginable because God is transcendent and not a big person in the sky. Nevertheless, God creating implies immediate presence because God creating out of nothing means nothing exists between finite reality and God creating. God creating is also ongoing, since creating is not an event of the past but the constant sustaining of temporal reality itself. This doctrine fits well with a scientific and historicist worldview because God creating does not amount to interventionism; God does not enter the world as a finite actor. God is the invisible power within everything that sustains it in being. More adequate conceptions of God use metaphors such as "ground of being" and "pure act of being" to curtail anthropomorphic images of God as a person in space or as locatable beyond it.

The conception of God as Creator has particular relevance for spirituality because it proposes the intrinsic presence of God to all created reality as its immediate power of being. This immediacy combines with the impossibility of separating God's creating from the idea of God loving what God creates that underlies the Jewish and Christian faith traditions. The intrinsic bond or identity of God's motive and God's action portray God as a loving Presence, a graceful God whose bearing toward all reality is favor and benediction. God is just such a Presence filling all of reality, all of nature. When the evolutionary process of life produced consciousness, there gradually arose a reflective species that could recognize and respond to that love. This hasty description provides an imaginary framework of a grace-filled naturalism that can carry Luther's spirituality into a present-day worldview.

*Jesus Christ centers Christian spirituality.* More has to be said to preserve the central role that Jesus Christ plays in Luther's spirituality within the transition to a framework of evolutionary creation. Spirituality in all faith traditions has a historical grounding: a point of departure in a particular historical milieu, a focusing event, and a contextual ambiance that fills out its meaning. For Christianity, Jesus of Nazareth, experienced as Christ or Messiah, fills that role for Christian faith and spirituality. Within the all-encompassing Jewish framework that situates Jesus and his teaching, and transcending the interpretations that Paul contributed to Christian understanding of Jesus, the person of Jesus and his teachings center the imaginations of Christians and their relationships with God and the world. The name of "Christian" spirituality is not wrong; the object of Christian faith is the transcendent Creator God, but the content and shape of Christian response to God is mediated and symbolized by Jesus interpreted as Christ. This content of Christian faith and spirituality defines the meaning of the term "Christomorphism." There is no naked faith in God as Creator. The notions of both God and God creating exist within a faith tradition. Jesus provides the form or contours of Christian faith and spirituality and gives focus to the notion of God.

This understanding helps to bring Luther's sixteenth-century spirituality into present-day culture without losing anything substantial from his own language. It allows for an acceptance of other revelations of God while explaining the distinctiveness of Christian faith and spirituality. It recognizes the particularity of the Jesus event and the Christian tradition while at the same time relating these to universal religious questions about the rationale and purpose of human existence itself. Jesus added his own appropriation of the Jewish tradition of faith in the

Creator God, so that his person and his teaching became the centering element of Christian spirituality. In Luther's language, the distinctive element in Christian spirituality is clinging to Christ as the one who introduces God to human consciousness, tutors the spiritual imagination, and points the direction of Christian life in the world toward love of neighbor.[3]

## A Spirituality of Gratitude

This interpretation of the spirituality of Martin Luther concludes with a consideration of its internal logic. After showing how his spiritual theology can be adjusted to life in a secular, scientific, and religiously plural culture, this final discussion characterizes Luther's spirituality as structured by the fundamental theological attitude of gratitude. This appreciation can be stated briefly and yet coherently by explaining the meaning of the theological attitude of gratitude, how it functions in Luther's spirituality, and how it might be deployed in the refocused way that fits today's culture.

*A fundamental theological attitude.* This idea of a fundamental theological attitude is constructed by analogy from the description of basic moral attitudes by Dietrich von Hildebrand.[4] His thinking is based on a theory of values. A value in this conception refers to something objective that bears the quality of being "important in itself." There are different kinds of values, such as aesthetic, moral, or intellectual, and even the ontological value of being itself that every entity exhibits. Objective values elicit a response that corresponds to their inherent quality or character. Response to values may be spontaneous but they emerge out of conscious perception and responsible freedom. Value response requires openness and appreciation and cannot be confused with need, usefulness, satisfaction, or fulfillment. The recognition and response to value find their basis and essential element in reverence. "Reverence is the presupposition for every response to value, every abandonment to something important."[5]

A fundamental moral attitude refers to a value response that is broad and capacious and has deepened to shape a person's consistent responses to reality. It resembles a Thomistic virtue, a disposition that enables or facilitates acts of responding to various forms of the good in a distinct way. Moral attitudes become resident qualities of the human spirit that together provide the basis for the moral life of the person.

The idea of a fundamental or basic theological and spiritual attitude extrapolates from this phenomenology of moral life and transfers the categories to theological perception and spiritual response. An examination of the basic logic of Luther's understanding of Christian spirituality finds that gratitude is its driving force. Surely faith is the supposition of Christian spirituality; faith designates the foundational perception out of which Christian life emerges. But the character of the religious and spiritual response takes the form of gratitude for God's initiative that is gratuitous and based on altruistic love, and that solicits a corresponding response of love in return. Faith provides the existential sphere within which this transpires.

*Gratitude in Luther's spirituality.* The term gratitude appears often enough in Luther's description of justification by grace through faith. But it does not get the same attention that he gives to faith. The reason for that is evident: his early work, which contains his strongest delineation of his conception of the Christian life, is polemically directed against a works spirituality. He himself was frustrated by a works spirituality; he witnessed it taking an overt, mechanical, and social form in a program for raising money. Faith as basic trust thus takes on an existential quality that appears to control or absorb all the energy of the Christian life. But a more careful look at how Luther explains the necessary role of human actions or works in Christian spirituality shows how gratitude motivates the Christian life. God's address to each person in Jesus Christ, perceived in faith as a forgiveness and mercy that totally accepts persons as they are individually, elicits or moves the response. Faith's perception of God's act of love for each person moves that person to respond in gratitude.

*Gratitude in a theocentric Christian creation spirituality.* Luther clearly specifies how God's love has visited humanity in Jesus Christ; God's love comes to humanity through Christ. But if Luther's christocentrism can be shifted to theocentrism, so too can creation theology generate massive gratitude. No one expresses this more forcefully than Ignatius of Loyola in the opening and closing meditations of his *Spiritual Exercises.* The *Exercises* essentially are a series of contemplations on Jesus's ministry, death, and resurrection. But they are bookended by an introductory meditation on the divine purpose in creating human beings and a conclusion to engender love of God in response for all God does for human beings in creation. Consider creation itself, Ignatius asks, and see God's love for each person manifested in their identity and their talents. God is at work in all of nature and history and pointedly for each one. Notice, he says, how "all good things and gifts descend from above; for example, my limited power from the Supreme and Infinite Power above; and so of justice, goodness, piety, mercy, . . . just as the rays come down from the sun, or the rains from their source."[6]

The positive power and driving force of gratitude comes to the surface in the spirituality of both Luther and Ignatius. Gratitude formulates what appears in consciousness as a kind of direct all-encompassing spiritual response that inspires and motivates Christian works. Of course, one can give reasons for one's gratitude, but the response exceeds them in a free interpersonal imperative. The reasons are not persuasive in themselves; they merely point to the gifts. The gift character of what is given, a manifestation of love, becomes the motive for response. The gifts to a person impel a relationship with the gift-giver in a bond of gratitude that, once given, cannot be erased. Both Luther and Ignatius insist that love and action are wedded together; love cannot be real without manifesting itself in action. The action of God's love thus stimulates a love in return, so that "works" or actions of love of neighbor as friends of God manifest the authenticity of a response to God. Luther's personalist theology and spirituality are sometimes characterized as individualist. In these texts the personal bond with God releases energy for love of neighbor in society that, like good fruit, reflect the character of the tree.

Luther's spirituality would never have been able to sustain a church tradition if it did not reflect some distinct yet fundamental dimension of Christian experience. Rather than being found in a single particular experience or virtue, this had to be something profound, essential, comprehensive, and integrating. The formula of justification by grace through existential faith points to that center of gravity. And deep inside the drama or narrative of that experience of transcendent acceptance and ratification of a person, gratitude plays a central role in motivating Christian spirituality.

## Notes

1. See John Thiel, "Tradition and Authoritative Reasoning: A Nonfoundationalist Perspective," *Theological Studies* 56 (December 1995), 627–51.

2. The concept as it is used here is drawn from Edward Schillebeeckx, who drew it from critical theory. See Edward Schillebeekx, *Church: The Human Story of God* (New York: Crossroad, 1990), 5–6. "I attach a great deal of importance to negative dialectics in general and . . . I have given particular attention to this concept in the work of the Frankfurt school. It has, however, always been my aim to stress the fact that these negative dialectics are sustained by a positive sphere of meaning which will direct praxis, even though this can only be expressed in a pluralist way." Edward Schillebeeckx, *The Understanding of*

*Faith: Interpretation and Criticism* (New York: Seabury Press, a Crossroad Book, 1974), 127.

3. This analysis raises the question of the uniqueness of Jesus relative to other religious mediators, an issue that has become acute in an age where religious pluralism appears to be intrinsic to human history. This issue cannot be addressed meaningfully in this context yetremains a topic of fruitful spiritual discussion.

4. The appeal here is to Dietrich von Hildebrand, *Fundamental Moral Attitudes* (New York: Longmans, Green and Co., 1950). See *Hildegard of Bingen and Francis of Assisi* in this series where the idea of a fundamental moral attitude is used to interpret the radicality of Francis.

5. von Hildebrand, *Fundamental*, 5, 11–12. "The capacity to grasp values, to affirm them, and to respond to them, is the foundation for realizing the moral values of man."

6. Ignatius of Loyola, *The Spiritual Exercises of Saint Ignatius*, trans. and commentary George E. Ganss (Chicago: Loyola Press, 1992), 95. There are more similarities between Luther and Ignatius than the mere fact that both are proposing Christian spiritualities. Interpretation has so emphasized reformation and counter currents that it often fails to see the many correlations and mutual enhancements that dialogue between them delivers. For example, Ignatius's preoccupation with sin in the first week of the Exercises is meant to stimulate an experience of God's love and forgiveness in response to sin and bears a close analogy with the dynamics of conversion in Luther.

## Further Reading

Brecht, Martin. *Martin Luther, I–III*. Philadelphia: Fortress Press, 1985–93. (A thorough treatment of the life and work of Martin Luther as it developed in context.)

Cameron, Euan K. *The European Reformation*. Oxford, New York: Oxford University Press, 2012. (Provides a realistic and balanced view of Europe and the church in it during the first half of the sixteenth century that enables an objective reading of Luther.)

Hendrix, Scott. *Martin Luther: Visionary Reformer*. New Haven and London: Yale University Press, 2015. (Presents a thorough, even-handed portrait of the many facets of Luther's life and thought.)

Hillerbrand, Hans J., et al., eds. *The Annotated Luther, I–VI*. Minneapolis: Fortress Press, 2015–17. (Six volumes of revised translations and new introductions to many of the classic works of Luther across a spectrum of topics that seek to open up his thought to a global audience. Luther's "On Christian Freedom" appears in vol. I with reader-friendly notes and commentary.)

Kaufmann, Thomas. *A Short Life of Martin Luther*. Grand Rapids: Eerdmans, 2016. (Kaufmann tells the complex story of Martin Luther and describes his theological teachings and how they were received in his time.)

Kolb, Robert. *Martin Luther: Confessor of the Faith*. Oxford, New York: Oxford University Press, 2009. (A reliable account of the early life of Luther, his conversion to reform, and the paradigm shifts that he introduced into theology and spirituality.)

McKim, Donald K., ed. *The Cambridge Companion to Martin Luther*. Cambridge: Cambridge University Press, 2003. (Eighteen essays on the life of Luther, the theological and ethical work of the reformer, and his influence on church and society in our time. Available online.)

Nelson, Derek, and Paul Hinlicky, eds. *The Oxford Encyclopedia of Martin Luther*. New York: Oxford University Press, 2017. (A comprehensive reference book that responds to the many questions that people might ask today about this classic reformer.)

Troeltsch, Ernst. "Lutheranism," *The Social Teaching of the Christian Churches*. New York: Harper Torchbook, 1960: 515–76. (A classic interpretation of the social dynamics of Luther's theology in the context of the church in sixteenth century Europe.)

## About the Series

The volumes of this series provide readers direct access to important voices in the history of the faith. Each of the writings has been selected, first, for its value as a historical document that captures the cultural and theological expression of a figure's encounter with God. Second, as "classics," the primary materials witness to the "transcendent" in a way that has proved potent for the formation of Christian life and meaning beyond the particularities of the setting of its authorship.

Recent renewed interest in mysticism and spirituality have encouraged new movements, contributed to a growing body of therapeutic-moral literature, and inspired the recovery of ancient practices from Church tradition. However, the meaning of the notoriously slippery term "spirituality" remains contested. The many authors who write on the topic have different frameworks of reference, divergent criteria of evaluation, and competing senses of the principal sources or witnesses. This situation makes it important to state the operative definition used in this series. *Spirituality is the way people live in relation to what they consider to be ultimate.* So defined, spirituality is a universal phenomenon: everyone has one, whether they can fully articulate it or not. Spirituality emphasizes lived experience and concrete expression of one's principles, attitudes, and convictions, whether rooted in a defined tradition or not. It includes not only interiority and devotional practices but also the real outworkings of people's ideas and values. Students of spirituality examine the way that a person or group conceives of a meaningful existence through the practices that orient them toward their horizon of deepest meaning. What animates their life? What motivates their truest desires? What sustains them and instructs them? What provides for them a vision of the good life? How do they define and pursue truth? And how do they imagine and work to realize their shared vision of a good society?

The "classic" texts and authors presented in these volumes, though they represent the diversity of Christian traditions, define their ultimate value in God through Christ by the Spirit. They share a conviction that the Divine has revealed God's self in history through Jesus Christ. God's self-communication, in turn, invites a response through faith to participate in an intentional life of self-transcendence and to co-labor with the Spirit in manifesting the reign of God. Thus, *Christian spirituality refers to the way that individuals or social entities live out their encounter with God in Jesus Christ by a life in the Spirit.*

Christian spirituality necessarily involves a hermeneutical task. Followers of Christ set about the work of integrating knowledge and determining meaning through an interpretative process that refracts through different lenses: the life of Jesus, the witness of the scripture, the norms of the faith community, the traditions and social structures of one's heritage, the questions of direct experience, the criteria of the academy and other institutions that mediate truthfulness and viability, and personal conscience. These seemingly competing authorities can leave contemporary students of theology with more quandaries than clarity. Thus, this series has anticipated this challenge with an intentional structure that will guide students through their encounter with classic texts. Rather than providing commentary on the writings themselves, this series invites the audience to engage the texts with an informed sense of the context of their authorship and a dialog with the text that begins a conversation about how to make the text meaningful for theology, spirituality, and ethics in the present. Most of the readers of these texts will be familiar with critical historical methods which enable an understanding of scripture in the context within which it was written. However, many people read scripture according to the common sense understanding of their ordinary language. This almost inevitably leads to some degree of misinterpretation. The Bible's content lies embedded in its cultural context, which is foreign to the experience of contemporary believers. Critical historical study enables a reader to get closer to an authentic past meaning by explicitly attending to the historical period, the situation of the author, and other particularities of the composition of the text. For example, one would miss the point of the story of the "Good Samaritan" if one did not recognize that the first-century Palestinian conflict between Jews and Samaritans makes the hero of the Jewish parable an enemy and an unlikely model of virtue! Something deeper than a simple offer of neighborly love is going on in this text.

However, the more exacting the critical historical method becomes, the greater it increases the distance between the text and the present-day reader. Thus, a second obstacle to interpreting classics for contemporary theology, ethics, and spirituality lies in a bias that texts embedded in a world so different from today cannot carry an inner authority for present life. How can we find something both true and relevant for faith today in a witness that a critical historical method determines to be in some measure alien? The basic problem has two dimensions: how do we appreciate the past witnesses of our tradition on their own terms, and, once we have, how can we learn from something so dissimilar?

Most Christians have some experience navigating this dilemma through biblical interpretation. Through Church membership, Christians have gained familiarity with scriptural language, and preaching consistently applies its content to daily life. But beyond the Bible, a long history of cultural understanding, linguistic innovation, doctrinal negotiations, and shifting patterns of practices has added layer upon layer of meaning to Christian spirituality. Veiled in unfamiliar grammar, images, and politics, these texts may appear as cultural artifacts suitable only for scholarly treatments. How can a modern student of theology understand a text cloaked in an unknown history and still encounter in it a transcendent faith that animates life in the present? Many historical and theological aspects of Christian spirituality that are still operative in communities of faith are losing traction among swathes of the population, especially younger generations. Their premises have been called into question; the metaphors are dead; the symbols appear unable to mediate grace; and the ideas appear untenable. For example, is the human species really saved by the blood of Jesus on the cross? What does it mean to be resurrected from the dead? How does the Spirit unify if the church is so divided? On the other hand, the positive experiences and insights that accrued over time and added depth to Christian spirituality are being lost because they lack critical appropriation for our time. For example, has asceticism been completely lost in present-day spirituality or can we find meaning for it today? Do the mystics live in another universe, or can we find mystical dimensions in religious consciousness today? Does monasticism bear meaning for those who live outside the walls?

This series addresses these questions with a three-fold strategy. The historical first step introduces the reader to individuals who represent key ideas, themes, movements, doctrinal developments, or remarkable distinctions in theology, ethics, or spirituality. This first section will equip readers with a sense of the context of the authorship and a grammar for understanding the text.

Second, the reader will encounter the witnesses in their own words. The selected excerpts from the authors' works have exercised great influence in the history of Christianity. Letting these texts speak for themselves will enable readers to encounter the wisdom and insight of these classics anew. Equipped with the necessary background and language from the introduction, students of theology will bring the questions and concerns of their world into contact with the world of the authors. This move personalizes the objective historical context and allows the existential character of the classic witness to appear. The goal is not the study of the exact meaning of ancient texts, as important as that is. That would require a task outside the scope of this series. Recommended readings will be provided for those who wish to continue digging into this important part of interpretation. These classic texts are not presented as comprehensive representations of their authors but as statements of basic characteristic ideas that still have bearing on lived experience of faith in the twenty-first century. The emphasis lies on existential depth of meaning rather than adequate representation of an historical period which can be supplemented by other sources.

Finally, each volume also offers a preliminary interpretation of the relevance of the author and text for the present. The methodical interpretations seek to preserve the past historical meanings while also bringing them forward in a way that is relevant to life in a technologically developed and pluralistic secular culture. Each retrieval looks for those aspects that can open realistic possibilities for viable spiritual meaning in current lived experience. In the unfolding wisdom of the many volumes, many distinct aspects of the Christian history of spirituality converge into a fuller, deeper, more far-reaching, and resonant language that shows what in our time has been taken for granted, needs adjustment, or has been lost (or should be). The series begins with fifteen volumes but, like Cassian's *Conferences*, the list may grow.

## About the Editors

ROGER HAIGHT is a visiting professor at Union Theological Seminary in New York. He has written several books in the area of fundamental theology. A graduate of the University of Chicago, he is a past president of the Catholic Theological Society of America.

ALFRED PACH III is an Associate Professor of Medical Sciences and Global Health at the Hackensack Meridian School of Medicine. He has a PhD from the University of Wisconsin in Madison and an MDiv in Psychology and Religion from Union Theological Seminary.

AMANDA AVILA KAMINSKI is an Assistant Professor of Theology at Texas Lutheran University, where she also leads the faith, diversity, and culture track in Social Innovation and Social Entrepreneurship. She has written extensively in this area of Christian spirituality.

Past Light on Present Life:
Theology, Ethics, and Spirituality

*Roger Haight, SJ, Alfred Pach III,*
and *Amanda Avila Kaminski,* series editors

**Available titles:**

*Western Monastic Spirituality: John Cassian, Caesarius of Arles,*
*and Benedict*
*On the Medieval Structure of Spirituality: Thomas Aquinas*
*Grace and Gratitude: Spirituality in Martin Luther*

Printed in the USA
CPSIA information can be obtained
at www.ICGtesting.com
JSHW021939260923
49097JS00024B/42